The Book of the
HONDA 90

A practical guide to the handling and maintenance of all Honda 90's up to 1966

John Thorpe

ANNOUNCEMENT

By special arrangement with the original publishers of this book, Sir Isaac Pitman & Son, Ltd., of London, England, we have secured the exclusive publishing rights for this book, as well as all others in THE MOTORCYCLIST'S LIBRARY.

Included in THE MOTORCYCLIST'S LIBRARY are complete instruction manuals covering the care and operation of respective motorcycles and engines; valuable data on speed tuning, and thrilling accounts of motorcycle race events. See listing of available titles elsewhere in this edition.

We consider it a privilege to be able to offer so many fine titles to our customers.

FLOYD CLYMER

Publisher of Books Pertaining to Automobiles and Motorcycles

2125 W. PICO ST.   LOS ANGELES 6, CALIF.

Preface

WITH the introduction of the 90 c.c. range of machines—and especially with the S.90 sports motor-cycle and the CM.90 scooter—Honda have significantly widened what was already a considerable appeal on the British market. Where, previously, there was a gap between the 50 and 125 c.c. motor-cycles there is now an intermediate range to cater for the rider who wants extra power but not the weight or complication of a "twin." And the scooterist who sought more power than even the astonishing Honda 50 could offer now has a mount which will bear comparison with established 100 c.c.—or even 125 c.c.—machines.

This extension of the range now means that the Hondas will appeal to an even wider public and is another milestone on the road travelled by this remarkable Japanese firm since their motor-cycles first became available here in the early sixties. In that short time, the Honda has become one of that rare band of machines able to excite in their owners a deep and lasting loyalty. This is a rare quality even among sports models; and when it has been done with bread-and-butter mounts also—as with Honda—it argues a considerable virtuosity in design and construction. That, of course, the Honda has.

It would perhaps be true to say that the Honda is the machine which, more than any other, has changed public thinking. How many of us, even five years ago, would have said that the man in the street would purchase a machine whose engine revved at 10,000 r.p.m.? But that is just what he does when he buys a Honda. More significantly, it is what the woman in his life does too. Why? Because Honda have proved that not only can a high-revving small power unit be made to produce a performance out of all relation to its nominal size, but also that it can be made utterly reliable and long-lasting.

Right from the start, Honda have sought to demonstrate that performance and reliability need not be mutually exclusive—as long as the factory has done its part of the job properly. On entering the U.K. market with the 50 c.c. machines, they started with a non-stop seven day run, at the Goodwood motor racing circuit, with three small Hondas covering 5,897, 5,023 and 4,935 miles respectively. Packing an average year's mileage into a week, they averaged between 30 and 35 m.p.h., and returned fuel consumptions of 124–140 m.p.g., Deservedly, they were awarded the Maudes Trophy for this fine performance.

This adventurous approach was in evidence in their relations with the Press, too. At that time I had one of the first batch of C.100 Hondas for road test—and Honda's challenge to me was as simple and direct as a journalist could ever hope to have from a manufacturer. "Break it if you can," they said. So I tried. I covered 2,200 miles. I beat every personal 50 c.c. point-to-point best time I had ever established in over a dozen years' motor-cycle journalism—and beat them by margins so large as to be almost ridiculous. For example, on a 35-mile run into Central London the Honda—with only 50 miles on the clock—bettered my previous 50 c.c. "best" by 13 minutes! When it was run in, it regularly reduced the original time by 20 minutes. Never had I previously ridden a machine which so obviously outclassed the opposition. . . .

That Honda didn't break. Nor did the later "50," which was subjected to the longest road test I have ever carried out—over a period of a year. That's the sort of machines they are; and the 90s are the same only more so. . . .

The private owner, however, does not set out to break his machine. That's where this book comes in. You *can* neglect your Honda and it will keep going. But give it the attention which is its right, and it will do more than that—it will keep going on top line. In the chapters which follow, I have included all the advice and data which is necessary to keep the machine well serviced; to trace any faults which do happen to arise; and to carry out basic overhaul procedures. I have not told you how to strip the engine to the last nut and bolt, because that is better left to the professionals. And, in any case, if you follow all the routine set out in the book you won't *need* to strip the engine to the last nut and bolt!

Once again, I feel that I must record my gratitude to Honda (U.K.) Ltd.—and especially to Sales Director Jim Harrisson—for the immediate and willing help they have given me in its compilation. Every facility for which I have asked has been cheerfully granted, including permission to use illustrations and material from the official workshop manuals.

The book covers all the 90 c.c. machines—the S.90 o.h.c. motor-cycle; the CM.90 o.h.v. scooter; and the C.200 o.h.v. motor-cycle—and I have also included the S.65 o.h.c. machine. Overseas owners will find that much of the data is also applicable to the 90 c.c. "Trail" 'bike and to the C.65 scooterette, neither of which are marketed in Britain.

For the CM.90 o.h.c. scooter, readers should follow the general instructions given for the S.90 engine, save for the automatic clutch, which is of CM.90 type.

JOHN THORPE

Contents

1 Meet the Honda 90

It is doubtful whether a machine has ever been introduced into Britain —or into any other country, come to that—which so immediately outclassed the opposition as did the original 50 c.c. Hondas. Their performance forced one to adopt entirely new standards for their capacity class.

Even so, give a man power and he will immediately want more. Hence, even the ample performance of the ultra-light Hondas did not satisfy some potential customers, and the logical outcome was that the basically similar but more powerful "90" was introduced. It came, first, in motorcycle form as the C.200—a mount which obviously owed much in general layout to the C.114, its 50 c.c. stablemate, whose frame and fork layout it shared. And, like the earlier machines, it also set new standards by outclassing machines with engines nearly half as big again.

This it seems is a Honda tradition, for the C.200's scooter counterpart— the CM.90—was hailed on its introduction as a direct challenge in the 125 c.c. scooter class. Surely no better compliment could ever be paid to a machine whose cubic capacity is precisely 86·7 c.c., and consequently much closer to the 50 c.c. class than to a "125"? Hondas, it seems, are now expected as a matter of course to be able to outclass their competitors.

In both cases, the formula with these "bread and butter" 90s has been to use the larger engine mounted in a frame basically identical to that of the 50 c.c. models, though with larger tyres and with detail variations. Since the Honda cycle parts are of pressed steel and are amongst the toughest made this is an excellent policy. But there was also a brand-new machine to come—the S.90—which was new from stem to stern.

This lively little mount is one of Honda's most inspired designs. Its 89·6 c.c. engine has a light alloy head, barrel and crankcase, and valve operation is by a chain-driven overhead camshaft. Running on a fairly modest compression ratio of 8·2 : 1, it produces 8 b.h.p. at 9,500 r.p.m. and is capable of bettering 60 m.p.h. on level roads. It has a specially-designed frame (Fig. 1), with telescopic front forks, to give handling in keeping with its sports specification.

To this 90 c.c. range, an intermediate machine was also added. This is the S.65, which uses a 65 c.c. version of the all-alloy o.h.c. engine in a frame akin to that of the C.200, forming an all-purpose motor-cycle with more performance than the "50s" and more refinement than the o.h.v. 90. It could best be regarded, in fact, as the touring equivalent of the

S.90. Finally, there came the o.h.c. version of the CM.90, with an S.90-type upper half.

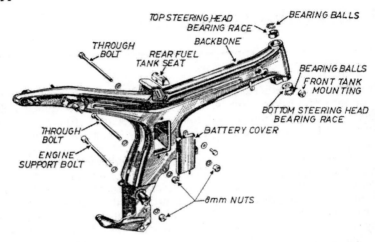

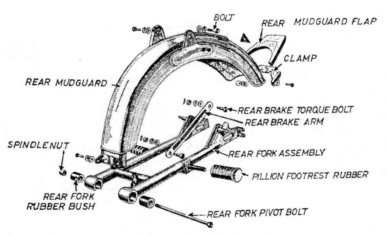

FIG. 1. THE S.90 FRAME

This sturdy pressed-steel frame, with tubular rear fork, is typical of modern Honda practice. It ensures a rigid steering head with consequent good steering.

As is standard Honda practice, all their motor-cycles have foot-controlled four-speed gearboxes, the ratios varying according to the engine characteristics and the purpose of the machine. In the case of the scooter, however, the highly-successful formula already used on the C.100 is repeated—a three-speed gearbox is combined with a fully-automatic clutch.

Again, following standard Honda practice, each machine is supplied very fully equipped with wing mirrors, flashing indicators, steering head lock, and so forth. Battery-boosted electrical systems are fitted to all models in this range, but none has an electric starter.

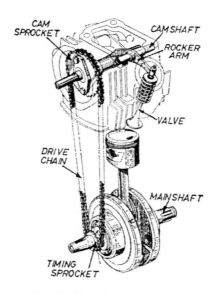

FIG. 2. THE O.H.C. SYSTEM

How the valves on the S.90 and S.65 models are operated by a chain driven direct from the main shaft.

Providing one has selected the right model to start with, any one of these machines will give superlative service. The great all-rounder, obviously, is the C.200 which, with 6½ h.p. and a four-speed gearbox, is a true "go-anywhere" mount. The CM.90's automatic clutch makes it eminently suitable for use in heavy traffic, and its ample mudguarding and shielding make it a highly practical machine for the rider who doesn't want to "dress up" to ride. I would also regard it as being the ideal "stand-by" mount for the car owner who finds himself becoming more and more frustrated by traffic jams and parking problems.

The S.90 is, obviously, for the man who likes a machine with a sporting flavour. More particularly, it should be an ideal "advanced trainer" for younger riders whose particular dream of bliss will eventually be the

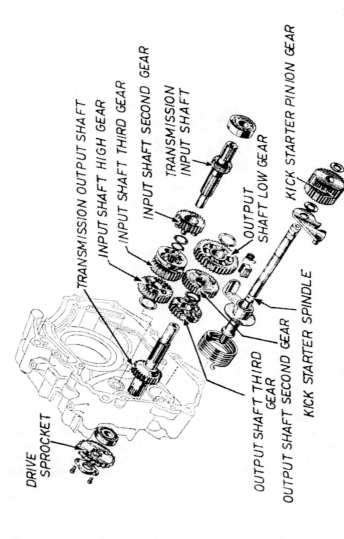

DRIVE SPROCKET

TRANSMISSION OUTPUT SHAFT

INPUT SHAFT HIGH GEAR

INPUT SHAFT THIRD GEAR

INPUT SHAFT SECOND GEAR

TRANSMISSION INPUT SHAFT

OUTPUT SHAFT LOW GEAR

KICK STARTER PINION GEAR

OUTPUT SHAFT THIRD GEAR

OUTPUT SHAFT SECOND GEAR

KICK STARTER SPINDLE

FIG. 3. THE S.90 GEARBOX

In construction, this is similar to all the four-speed Honda gearboxes

305 c.c. Super Sports or even the mile-eating "450." The S.65, on the other hand, would be the obvious first step towards, say, the C.72 range.

Certainly, all these machines offer both excellent value for money and excellent performance out of all proportion to their nominal size. Not only that, a Honda is a good investment. It is a high-quality machine, and experience has shown that depreciation is less than with most other mounts of comparable price. The advice and working instructions given in this book are designed to help you keep your Honda on top line, and to get the most out of it in terms of performance, reliability and enjoyment.

2 Handling your Honda

IT is, perhaps, a tribute to the inherent simplicity and safety of the light-weight scooter or motor-cycle that a tradition has arisen that nobody needs to be taught how to handle it. Newcomers to cars may need twelve hours or so of professional instruction. Would-be pilots in relatively uncrowded skies—who may make a couple of control corrections in a 50-mile flight—require 40 hours tuition. Even for the highly unmechanical sailing boat several hours teaching is called for. But for a novice, just showing them the two-wheeler's controls is thought to be sufficient as a rule.

It may be true enough that, where the machine concerned is as well designed and built as a Honda, mere self-tuition should leave a pretty reasonable safety factor. But with the growing congestion on the roads and the increasing number of laws and restrictions it is no longer the best way to do so.

In some parts of the country, it is no longer necessary either. These are areas where the R.A.C./A.-C.U. Learner Training Scheme is operated. Riding and mechanical instruction is given by members of motor-cycle clubs—real enthusiasts, who love the game and are happy to pass on their knowledge to the newcomer so that he, too, will become as enthusiastic as he is proficient.

Under the Scheme, all the initial instruction takes place on private ground, and no pupil is taken out until the instructor thinks that a minimum standard of proficiency has been reached. At the end of the course a certificate of proficiency can be gained and, though this does not absolve one from taking the rather sketchy and haphazard M.o.T. Driving Test, possession of this proof of one's ability is nevertheless a great morale-booster.

As yet, the Scheme does not operate everywhere, but there is a pretty constant expansion, and the Manager of the R.A.C. Motor-cycle Department, 85 Pall Mall, London, S.W.1, is always prepared to put inquirers into touch with the nearest centre.

Where no Scheme exists, self-tuition must, of necessity, fill the gap. The danger here is that bad riding habits may be formed quite unwittingly, and subsequently become very difficult to break. The style which you evolve in the early days of your roadfaring are likely to remain with you, substantially unchanged, through the rest of your life. It is this initial period which mainly determines whether you will become a safe, skilled and considerate rider or a mobile menace; and whether you understand and use your machine properly or become a mechanical wrecker. Much wear and tear on the bike—to say nothing of the rider—and a considerable amount of time and money-wasting tinkering can be saved by good riding habits.

Start your studies in an armchair, learning all about your Honda and its controls. Having memorized the location and operation of each of them—including the various switches controlling the main and dipped beams, horn, winkers and so forth—close your eyes and pretend you are on the bike. Then give yourself a series of quick tests; for example, "Apply the front brake," "Signal a right turn," "Dip the lights" and so forth. Make the appropriate hand or foot movement as quickly as you can after thinking of the action, so that eventually hand and brain act almost at the same instant. On the road, "thinking time" is dangerous time. At 30 m.p.h.—usually regarded as a pretty low speed—you cover 44 feet in each second. If you can cut your reaction time by even a quarter of a second, therefore, you save yourself 11 feet in total braking distance. That could be the difference between life and death.

With all the controls memorized and your armchair instruction at an end, go to your machine, put it on its stand, sit on it, and go through the exercises again—*with your eyes shut.* The reason is simple enough—on the road you haven't time to look for the controls. You must be able to reach and operate each one instinctively leaving your eyes free to watch the road ahead.

Your next step is to learn how to start the engine and how to keep it under control once it is going. Turn on the petrol and if the air temperature is low, also use the strangler.

Keep the machine on its stand and get astride. Switch on the ignition, having checked that the machine is in neutral, and open the twist-grip throttle by about an eighth of an inch. You don't need more than that—and too big a throttle opening may even prevent the engine starting. Now kick start the engine by placing the ball of your foot on the starter pedal and thrusting it downwards in an arc, keeping the pressure constant right to the end of the stroke. Don't just jab at it. Give a really steady thrust which will spin the motor properly. Your Honda will start within a couple of kicks and will idle reliably. Let it warm up for a minute or two, and then open the choke fully. This should be done as soon as the engine will run without the choke, since the richer mixture tends to accelerate engine wear.

Next, sit on your machine and spend a few minutes gently opening and closing the throttle so that you become accustomed to the way the unit responds. Here, again, concentrate on obtaining a smooth and progressive action. Don't jerk the throttle open—turn it a fraction of an inch at a time, noting how the engine speeds up as you do so. As there is no load it will tend to accelerate very quickly, so be careful. Don't let it race, or it may over-rev and damage its own valve gear. Use just enough throttle each time to accustom yourself to the "feel" of the control, so that when you come to ride your Honda you will be able to operate it smoothly and so avoid progressing in a series of kangaroo-like jerks.

Unless you have a CM.90, whose automatic clutch takes this particular worry off your shoulders, one of your main difficulties will be mastering the delicate art of co-ordinating the operation of the clutch and the throttle on take-off. Therefore, practice this before you start riding in earnest. Roll the Honda off its stand, start the engine and, sitting on the bike, pull the clutch lever right back to the handlebar. Engage first gear, and release the clutch lever by unfolding your left hand reasonably quickly, but smoothly, with the lever under full control of your hand all the time. As the lever gets about half-way back to its normal position you will feel the drive begin to take up, the machine tending to ease forward a little. This is the first stage of moving off—the drive being transmitted, yet with the clutch slipping so that the full load is not applied to the engine at a time when to do so would stall it.

As soon as you reach this point, withdraw the clutch again; select neutral; wait a minute; and then repeat the operation. The idea is to become accustomed to the "feel" of the drive taking up and checking the release of the clutch at that precise point. To hold the clutch out for very long would, however, overheat and perhaps burn out the plates. Hence the selection of neutral and the minute's interval to give the plates time to cool again before the lesson is repeated.

Once you can let out the clutch fairly rapidly as far as the take-up point and instantly check your hand movement there, you are ready to go on to the next stage—that is, to make an actual getaway. Carry out the exercise just described as far as checking the left hand. Then, instead of withdrawing the clutch, give just a little extra throttle—about another eighth to a quarter of an inch should suffice—and the machine will move off. Immediately, get both feet on the rests and as you do so slowly let the clutch full out, so that you are riding along in first gear. For this exercise it is best to have a reasonably long run in front of you, so that you can practise opening and closing the throttle and noting how the machine's speed responds to the various settings of the twist grip. You will find that within a few minutes you have become adept at controlling your speed by varying the position of the grip—back towards you for faster; away from you for slower.

Naturally, you will have to stop. Do this by closing the throttle, withdrawing the clutch, and appyling both brakes gently. As soon as the machine stops, drop the right foot to support it and with the other select neutral. Then hop off, wheel your machine round, and repeat the getaway and speed control exercises all the way back. Before long, you should be able to move off and stop smoothly, and vary the speed competently in between. You are then ready for the next stage—changing gear.

Move off as before and reach, say, 10 m.p.h. in first gear. Then at one and the same time snap the throttle shut and draw out the clutch. As you do so, operate the gear pedal to select second gear, releasing it as soon as you have moved it as far as it will go. Immediately, let the clutch go fully home. There's no need for a slow movement this time. The faster you get it back into engagement the better. You can now open the throttle again, and you will find that the machine will be pulling much as before but in a higher gear. One difference, though, will be that the response to the throttle will be noticeably slower than before, both in accelerating and in slowing down. So practise both until you have got the new "feel."

Repeat the same procedure to accustom yourself to both engaging second and changing back into first. When you feel that you are proficient, try bringing the other gears into play, until you can ride along going up and down through the box.

When engaging a higher gear, you always close the throttle. To make a smooth engagement into a lower gear—from top to third; or from second to first, for example—it is better to leave the throttle slightly open so that the engine can speed up and ease the engagement. This is the neatest way of doing it. Equally effective, if not so polished, is the method of giving a short "blip" on the throttle as the pedal is moved.

By now, you should also be able to make a turn in the road without hopping off the machine. This is done in first gear and after the necessary observation and signalling. It involves nothing more complicated than leaning the machine well over and letting it turn under power. If on your early attempts you find yourself running towards the kerb don't panic. Just lift the machine up, pull the clutch lever towards you, and operate the brakes. Before long, you'll be able to ride round in a circle in an average-width surburban road without even touching the clutch. It's merely a question of developing judgement.

With the CM.90, of course, all the clutchwork is done for you, and providing you don't make the mistake of holding the gear pedal down and so operating the over-ride device on the clutch all you need do is concentrate on clean throttle work. Honda automatic clutches are coupled in three ways—and one of these is to the gear pedal, so if the pedal is released sharply with the throttle open the result is a disconcerting "bunny jump."

When braking, whatever the type of machine, always use the two brakes in unison. If you like, you can give the front brake a slight "lead" over the rear. Try to cure yourself of any "rear brake only" complex inherited from cycling days. Whatever may have been the case with your bicycle, on a Honda the brakes are perfectly balanced and they are intended to be used together.

Naturally, you need to take care if the roads are slippery. Under such conditions, allow extra distance for slowing down, so that you can reduce the pressure applied to the brake controls and so keep well away from the situation in which they may lock because of over-powerful application.

You can often use the braking power of the engine in the lower gears for initial deceleration, reserving the brakes to "kill" the last few m.p.h. This reduces the risk of skidding.

When descending a steep hill, too, you can engage a lower gear to help keep the speed under control. This, plus the barest "tickle" on the front brake, is normally far more effective than descending with both brakes on.

As previously explained, your motor-cycle is steered by being inclined to one side or the other. From that, you will have gathered that to go round a corner you balance one upsetting force against another. It follows that the degree of bank adopted must be exactly proportional to the speed at which the corner is taken and the sharpness of the corner itself. The art of cornering a two-wheeler cannot be learned from a book. It demands constant practice. But concentrate upon taking corners on the right "line"—basically, a smooth sweep parallel to the kerb on slow corners or as near a straight line as can legally be contrived on fast ones. And in each case, learn to use the minimum amount of bank which will take you round. There is nothing clever in wearing away the rubber on your footrests by grounding them on mild corners. The machine is at its most stable when it is upright, and every degree of inclination which is not strictly necessary is merely eating into your safety margin. On very slippery roads, in fact, I prefer to keep the machine upright and counteract the rather low centrifugal forces involved by means of body lean—a trials-riding technique.

In general, then, incline the machine for the corner as much as you have to but no more. My preference is to accelerate round corners, but it is equally permissible to take them at a constant throttle opening. What is to be avoided at all costs, however, is to enter the corner too fast and then brake with the machine still banked. This will almost certainly result in a spill. If a corner has been misjudged, lift the bike upright as fast as you can and apply the brakes hard, while travelling straight, to lose as much speed as possible. If necessary—and assuming the road is clear—let it run on with the brakes applied until the proximity of a kerb or wall makes it imperative to swerve. Where the road is not clear, lose as much speed as possible and then release the brakes and bank again. Sometimes, one can take two or three "bites" at a corner in this way. But it is, of course, purely an emergency procedure and one which, if it has to be indulged in at all frequently, argues a decided lack of judgement which should be corrected.

3 The tools you need

It is a ludicrous mistake to spend over £100 on a quality mount and then let it depreciate by grudging an extra expenditure of perhaps £5 on the tools which will keep it in good order. And, the tool kit supplied with a Honda, even though it would put to shame those normally issued with most other makes, is really intended only for running repairs and general maintenance. For major work, it will pay to invest in a workshop kit, which over the years will more than repay its initial cost. You will change your motor-cycle, but your tool kit is there for good.

Specifically for the Honda, you will also need a certain number of special tools—a generator rotor puller, for example. Where such a tool is required, I have noted the fact in the text. Don't try to make do without it—Hondas are made to very fine limits indeed, and in these instances the special tool is designed to do a particular job without damaging the unit. It is no saving to keep a few shillings in your pocket by "improvising," when by doing so you may have halved the life of a component costing pounds to replace. So, if you haven't got the tool, don't do the job.

Spanners, screwdrivers and so forth are not special tools—but they are nonetheless essential ones. Buy the best that you can afford. Cheap tools are not really all that much cheaper, and they are neither as efficient nor as long-lasting. If you intend to become a real rider-mechanic (as most motor-cyclists do) get yourself a good set of chrome-vanadium spanners. Open-enders ranging from 8 mm to, say, 22 mm should be the first item on the list. Supplement these with a set of ring spanners—preferably ranging from 6 mm upwards. And when you can really afford to go to town, get a socket set too. This cannot replace either the rings or the open-enders, but these tools are the most versatile of them all. You can obtain all manner of accessories to go with them—long and short extensions; extension with universal joints so that you can operate round corners; ratchet wrenches which enable you to undo nuts with little more than flicks of the wrist; and a torque wrench which permits nuts and bolts to be tightened to an exact setting specified by the manufacturer.

If finances will not run to the socket set, you should at least obtain an assortment of stout box spanners and a really substantial tommy bar.

You will also need some additional screwdrivers. Excellent though the standard Honda screwdriver with its interchangeable blade is, my experience has been that it will not free really tight cross-headed screws. For this sort of job, the best answer is the workshop-type cross-headed screw-driver used by Honda mechanics. This has a T-head which gives ample leverage. In addition, a full kit should include a long-bladed and a short-bladed insulated electrical screwdriver; a pair of long-nosed pliers incorporating wire cutters and strippers; and a set of feeler gauges. For lubrication a pressure oil can is useful and a grease gun is vital. As an investment this should be of the high-pressure type (such as a Wanner) or if you prefer a lighter gun with cartridge loading (a Nubrex, for instance) one equipped with a high-pressure hose would be satisfactory. But a cheaper gun will do, since the Honda has only low pressure nipples.

A collection of clean tin boxes or a set of specially-made steel or plastic trays is useful for storing parts removed from the machine. Ideally, you should also have an inspection lamp, preferably of the clip-on type, since this will enable you to see what you are doing while leaving both hands free. On this score, too, a Mole wrench—which can be used almost as a portable vice—is a worthwhile addition to your kit.

Where you plan to do more than the usual amount of work on your machine you can, of course, expand your tool kit further. A selection of files of various cuts are near-essentials; as are soft-metal drifts; hardened punches; hard- and soft-faced hammers; a drill—preferably electric—with bits; and a workbench with a vice. But the great thing about a workshop is that it can be built up over the years. There's no need to obtain everything at once, yet once bought good tools last and are rarely wasted.

USING YOUR TOOLS

Even the simplest hand tools demand rather more than merely to be placed in position and tugged hard. Each type of spanner, for example, has its own purpose and its own characteristics.

Unquestionably the great all-rounders of the tool kit are the open-enders, which are slimly built and which can therefore be slipped into confined spaces which no other spanner could reach. Their jaws are angled. That means that the spanner can be used to loosen a nut when only a few degrees of movement are possible. When the limit has been reached, the tool is removed, reversed, and room for another few degrees of movement is thus obtained.

Naturally, only the right size of spanner should be used. The open-ender is designed to exert pressure along the flats of a nut or bolt and is consequently made with jaws of just the right width for the job. Use too large a spanner and it will sit at angle, applying the full force you exert not along the flats but on two of the angles. Normally, this stress is just too much for the metal of the bolt. The spanner turns, taking with it the two corners against which it was pressing, and you are left with a rounded head which no spanner will grip. Just occasionally, the bolt bites back and springs the jaws of the spanner instead. Then you have a ruined spanner. . . .

You can also damage the jaws by applying too much force when trying to free a stubborn bolt. Here, one is often tempted to slip a piece of piping over the spanner to increase the leverage, or link two spanners together by interlocking their jaws. The best advice is—don't. Such methods may succeed occasionally, but normally they will ruin either the bolt or the spanner, or both. There is, for instance, always a danger that the bolt may be snapped in two.

Instead, try a different type of spanner—a ring or a socket. These do not operate on the flats, but on the angles, and they therefore have the advantage of exerting pressure all round the head with no danger of slipping. The same pressure applied through a ring or a socket may do the trick. If not, try the effect of jarring the thread by placing a drift against the face of the bolt head and giving a sharp tap with a hammer. Repeat this half a dozen times. If it fails, give the bolt best for the time being and swamp it with penetrating oil. Repeat the dose at hourly intervals and you will, eventually, find that its grip has loosened. Where nuts or bolts are obviously rusted they should be soaked with penetrating oil some time before an attempt to loosen them is made.

Just as there is a knack in undoing nuts and bolts, so there is in tightening them. Excessive force should not be employed, and if a torque wrench can be used to tension them to an exact setting so much the better. Otherwise, exert only full hand pressure—not arm pressure—and do so through the length of the spanner alone, not through an artificially lengthened tool. Every spanner is made to a length appropriate to the size of the nut and bolt which it is to deal with, and use of too much force may lead to fractures.

This consideration applies particularly to Hondas, where light alloy plays a notable part in the construction. Here, the steel bolt is considerably harder than the alloy into which it is threaded, and over-enthusiasm with the spanners will rip the threads in the alloy. After that, you will need to retap the hole and use a larger bolt.

Pliers, of course, should never be used as makeshift spanners—they damage the hexagons—and adjustable spanners should be reserved for emergency use, since they can never be as accurately set as the correct spanner.

Screwdriver blades, too, should be appropriate to the size of the slot in the screw heads. Don't try to force a thick blade into a fine slot; nor use a thin blade in a wide one. Either way, you'll simply damage the head. With stubborn cross-headed screws, you will find that the driver tends to ride out of the cross. If this happens, place a drift on the screw and give it several sharp blows with a hammer. But be very careful if you are doing this on a light-alloy component, or you may fracture it. For really stubborn screws, try the effect of local heat on the alloy—a rag soaked in boiling water may do the trick. Again, penetrating oil might help.

After use, clean your tools before they are put away. Many mechanics like to wipe them with a lightly-oiled rag after the dirt has been cleaned off. This certainly helps to preserve the tools, but remember that any oil should be dried off before they are used again. Wrap them in clean dry rag—not in plastic sheeting, for this causes rusting—hang them up in racks in your workshop, or keep them in a special tool box. Whichever course you choose, make sure that they are stored in a dry place. They will then give you service as good as that of the Honda itself.

4 How to trace faults

IF, feeling off colour, you visit your doctor you do not expect him to treat you by haphazardly amputating your leg, your arm, or your tonsils. Were he to attempt to do so, you would soon be on the look-out for a new medical man. Yet not a few riders treat their machines in just that way— and apart from refusing to work altogether there is nothing that the long-suffering motor-cycle can do about it.

When an engine goes sick, or an electrical system breaks down, the way to cure it is to adopt the same approach that you would expect from your own doctor—a methodical examination, with all the symptoms weighed up, followed by a logical diagnosis which accords with the facts.

Take the engine first. Here you can make one basic assumption. If the correct charge of mixture is induced at the proper time; is compressed; is fired by a spark occurring at the correct instant; and if the residue is properly exhausted then the engine *must* work. If it is not working it proves that one of these basic requirements is not being met, and you must carry out an examination to discover why.

The first stage must be the obvious one—a check on the fuel supply. Is there fuel in the tank? If so, is it reaching the carburettor? You can test that easily enough by depressing the float chamber tickler and seeing if petrol floods from the carburettor after, say, 10 seconds. If it doesn't the fault is some form of fuel stoppage—you may even have forgotten to switch the tap on, or have failed to set it to "reserve" on a low supply. Or, a filter may be blocked. Detach the pipe from the carburrettor and see if petrol flows steadily through it. If it does, you know that the stoppage must be in the carburettor itself—and presumably in the needle valve. If it doesn't, or if the flow is intermittent, it can mean that the pipe is blocked; that the tap or filter is blocked; or that the fuel tank air vent in the cap is blocked (Fig. 4).

Check the pipe itself by detaching it from the tap and then moving the tap to the "on" position. If fuel emerges in a steady flow you obviously have a blocked fuel pipe on your hands—a proposition you can confirm by simply attempting to blow through the pipe with your mouth. If it is blocked, you can clear the stoppage by the judicious use of a piece of wire.

Where the pipe passes muster, check the cap vent by removing the cap altogether. The result should be a steady flow through the tap. Again, no flow means that the only other possibility—the blocked tap—is the

FIG. 4. THE FILLER VENT

This section through the S.90's filler cap shows how the tank is vented to the atmosphere, and so allows pressure above and below the fuel to be balanced. If the vents are blocked no fuel can leave the tank.

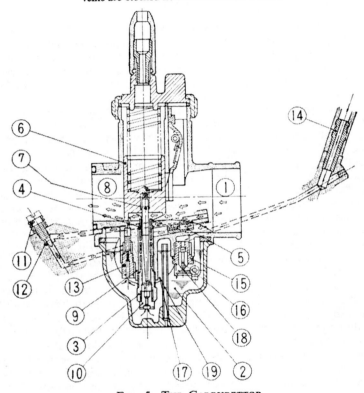

FIG. 5. THE CARBURETTOR

Arrowed, is the air flow through the carburettor fitted to the S.90. Although differing in detail construction all Honda carburettors work on the same principle and are of broadly similar design. The parts indicated are—

1. Venturi	11. Air screw
2. Float chamber	12. Passage
3. Needle jet holder	13. Slow-running jet
4. Needle jet	14. Fuel passage
5. Air jet	15. Float chamber needle valve body
6. Throttle slide	16. Needle
7. Jet needle	17. Float
8. Mixing chamber	18. Float-arm
9. Main jet threads	19. Overflow tube
10. Main jet orifice	

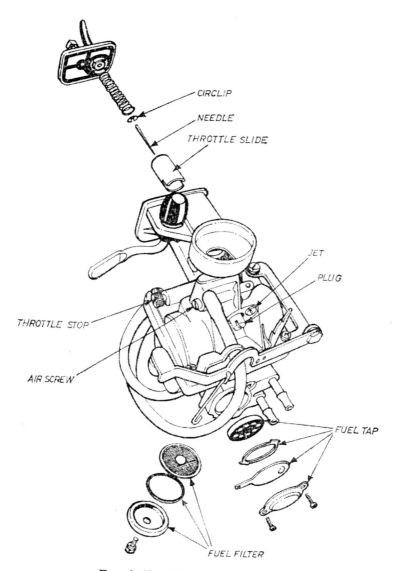

CIRCLIP

NEEDLE

THROTTLE SLIDE

JET

PLUG

THROTTLE STOP

AIR SCREW

FUEL TAP

FUEL FILTER

FIG. 6. THE CM.90 CARBURETTOR

Unusual in having the mixing chamber body set horizontally rather than vertically,
the Keihin carburettor used on the CM.90 is of otherwise straightforward construction. Note, however, that the fuel tap and the fue lfilter are both combined with
the carburettor.

answer. Clearing it will probably involve detaching the complete tap, and before doing so it is best to drain off all the fuel. You can prevent fuel loss, however, by completely sealing the filler orifice with cellulose tape.

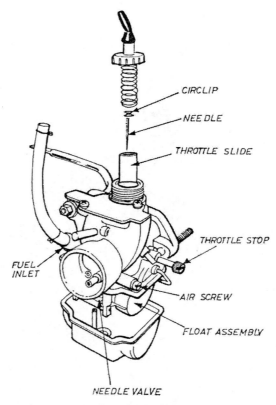

CIRCLIP

NEEDLE

THROTTLE SLIDE

THROTTLE STOP

FUEL INLET

AIR SCREW

FLOAT ASSEMBLY

NEEDLE VALVE

FIG. 7. THE S.90 CARBURETTOR

For the sports motor-cycle, Hondas employ a carburettor of this type. Note the extended throttle stop screw which normally projects beyond the carburettor casing. It is made by Mikuni.

If no air can enter no fuel can leave, and the tap can then be detached and opened up for cleaning.

Where the initial check showed that fuel was reaching the end of the pipe but not entering the carburettor, the next step would be to turn off the petrol and remove the carburettor for examination. The fault could only be a needle valve blocked with dirt—which could be cleaned by flushing it in petrol—or a valve which was jamming because of a mechanical fault. It might, for example, have been bent through careless re-assembly—by a previous owner, of course! Here, replacement by a new part would be the only viable course of action to take.

There are three other types of fuel problem. One is overflooding—

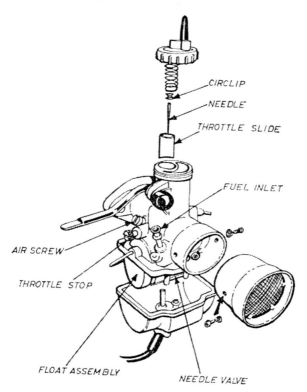

FIG. 8. THE C.200 CARBURETTOR

Similar in layout to the instrument on the sports machine, the C.200 carburettor is by Keihin. The major difference is in the design of the choke mechanism, the strangler slide (not shown here) moving vertically instead of pivoting.

evidenced by fuel dripping from the carburettor when the tap is switched on and by misfiring and lumpy running if the engine works at all. Again, only the float/needle valve assembly can be responsible for this. The valve may be prevented from closing by dirt; the float may be leaking, in which case it will not lift the needle enough to shut off the supply; or a damaged needle may not be seating properly. Check all three points.

Then there is failure of the fuel to pass through the jets. Again, the cause is likely to be dirt which has become trapped in the very fine passage which constitutes a jet. Such trouble often takes the form of an engine which will start, but which will not continue to run when the throttle is opened or which will run but which will not pull under load. Stripping out the jets and examining them is the obvious procedure. If you find one which is blocked, holding it to your lips and blowing though it in the reverse direction to that which the petrol flows in will normally dislodge the dirt. At a pinch, poke it clear with a bristle. You can in an emergency use a piece of thin wire, but this may easily damage the jet. Since it is not worth being stuck on a lonely road half the night for the sake of a sixpenny jet, I would certainly use whatever means were to hand to clear it and then replace the jet at the earliest opportunity thereafter.

Where an initial check on the fuel system discloses no obvious faults the next stage in fault tracing should be to test the ignition system and, more especially, to examine the sparking plug itself. To a knowledgeable rider the plug can often tell a revealing tale of conditions in the engine. If the nose of the plug is covered with soft black soot it usually means that the engine has been running over-rich. If, on the other hand, the nose and insulator have an ash-white appearance it denotes hot running, which in turn infers that the mixture is too weak. Here, one can again think in terms of fuel starvation and blocked jets. Hard glazed carbon on the plug shows that oil is being burned—possibly due to a worn bore, faulty rings or leakage down the inlet valve guide. But normal combustion is indicated by a coffee-coloured plug.

Your first sight of the plug, therefore, will have given you several clues about the conditions inside the engine. Closer examination will tell you more. If, for example, the plug has not been firing at all it is likely to be wet with fuel. But don't take that on trust. Even if it is dry, you should reconnect it to the H.T. lead, place it in contact with the metal of the cylinder, and switch on the ignition. Then, keeping the plug body well in contact with the engine, kick the unit over. A fat blue spark should jump across the gap between the plug's electrodes each time the kickstarter is operated. No spark indicates an ignition fault, and your next step is to find out exactly where it is. First of all, eliminate the plug itself from your list of suspects by fitting a brand-new plug in its place and carrying out the spark test all over again. If the new plug sparks the inference is pretty obvious. But, if there is still no spark, then the fault must be in the generator, the contact-breaker, the plug lead or the cap.

Even though the old plug sparked, the trouble may still be solved by fitting a new plug. The reason is that a plug which works when tested out of the engine may still be faulty when fitted and subjected to the pressures existing in the combustion chamber. Once the plug's efficiency has been established beyond all doubt, carry on by testing the plug lead.

To do this, you will need a long piece of wire—a nail even. Insert this so that it makes electrical contact in the plug cap, and position it so that it is about an eighth of an inch from the bare metal of the cylinder head or barrel. Keeping it there, operate the kickstarter. You should obtain a spark across the gap. If you fail to do so, unscrew the cap from the lead and jam the wire or nail into the hole in the centre of the lead into which the cap was screwed. Then repeat the test. Either you will get a spark or you won't. If you don't, then the fault lies deeper in the system. If you do, it proves that the cap was faulty. You can often cure this by cleaning the inside of the cap—this tends to accumulate dirt, which eventually leads to tracking—or, where it is already clean, by chopping a quarter of an inch or so off the H.T. lead so that the cap's screw bites into fresh core. Re-test after each operation.

Where the plug and cap have both been checked without result, turn your attention to the wiring. Test all leads and terminals for security and proper insulation. You should always carry with you your handbook containing the wiring diagram. Use this to help in your check on the wiring. The ignition switch itself may be faulty. Here, one indication is whether or not the neutral-indicator light comes on when the ignition switch is operated with the gears in neutral. If it does, it suggests that the switch is in order.

A complete electrical check by the wayside is, of course, out of the question. Only one immediate possibility remains—to test the contact-breaker and timing. With the points fully open, measure the gap between them. If it varies significantly from the recommended setting readjust them and see what effect this has. Clean them, too, by inserting a piece of clean card or paper and closing the points so that they just—but only just—grip it. Then carefully pull it out; select a fresh area; and repeat the operation until the paper is clean on withdrawal.

Lastly, check that the points are breaking at the correct setting. The timing marks will give you the datum which you need, and if there is any significant variation you can easily re-time the spark.

The only other "simple" fault which could cause such a complete electrical failure is saturation of the electrics with water—as might occur if the machine has been charged into a flooded patch. Here, the cure is to dry the system out by soaking up the moisture with clean rag. Otherwise, the conclusion must be that the fault is a fundamental one—failure of the coil, perhaps—which can only be tested and rectified by a garage.

Mechanical defects severe enough to lead to engine failure are rare indeed, and are likely to be the results of some other fault rather than first causes. On the other hand, they *will* stop the machine. . . . Failure to keep the oil level correct and to change the lubricant at the proper intervals can, for instance, lead to seizure and this, in turn, may break the rings. When that happens the compression will be insufficient to enable the mixture to be burned properly, and the engine will not run. Loss of compression can easily be felt through the kickstarter—there is little or no resistance as the engine is turned. Where broken rings are suspected it is essential that the engine should be turned over as little as possible, since the sharp ends of the snapped rings can play havoc with the surface of the bore, and can completely ruin it within minutes. Any sudden loss of power coupled with heavy blue smoke from the exhaust is likely to be due to ring breakage, and action should be taken accordingly.

A gradual loss of compression is more likely to be caused by a tappet which is tightening itself, and so holding one or other of the valves off its seat. If it is an inlet valve which is not seating properly the unit will tend to spit back through the carburettor. If an exhaust valve is affected there will probably be back-firing and rumbling in the exhaust. In either case, idling is almost certain to be unreliable and the unit will probably tend to overheat.

Running with a tight tappet can cause damage—and not just to the valve and its seat. Local overheating may distort the cylinder head/ barrel/crankcase joints and in severe cases may even result in a hole being melted through the crown of the piston. An emergency adjustment should therefore be made. It is impossible to set Honda tappets accurately with the engine hot, but you can at least ensure that the valve is freed by finding T.D.C. with both valves at rest and then setting the adjusters so that the tappets have just a slightly perceptible play with the valve fully seated. This is, of course, a "get you home" measure, and as soon as the unit is cold the proper settings should be made.

Blockage of either the indication or exhaust systems is highly unlikely, and providing both valves are seen to be operating and the compression is sound it can safely be assumed that mixture is being induced, compressed and the residue exhausted. That being so, any mechanical failure would be of the order of slipped valve timing or an actual breakage of a valve, spring, push rod or chain. None of those faults can be corrected at the roadside and garage assistance will therefore be needed.

Transmission faults are more straightforward—either the drive is being transmitted or it isn't, at least as a general rule. But mild clutch slip may sometimes give the impression that the engine is losing power. The easiest way to check this is to snap the throttle open on a steep gradient, listening very carefully to the exhaust note. If it rises sharply, but without the machine itself gaining speed, it is a sure sign of clutch slip. This can be caused only by maladjustment, or by worn plates or tired springs. If the adjustment proves to be correct then the clutch will have to be stripped for new parts to be fitted.

A process of elimination can also be applied to the lighting system. Here, the lamp *must* light if electricity is present and there is a full circuit. If it doesn't light, it proves that there is either no electricity or else a faulty circuit. I have found, from experience, that Japanese bulbs are not up to the engineering standard of Japanese engines. Bulbs which on visual examination seemed to be in good order were in fact duds, the wires inside the body having failed and caused an open circuit. Before going any further, therefore, I would always suggest substituting a new bulb for the original one to see if that is the part at fault. If it isn't, take the checking a stage further.

For this, you will need to have your wiring diagram so that the circuits can be traced. The fault for which you are looking may be one of two kinds—a short circuit or an open circuit. Electricity, as we have already noted, will always take the shortest path to earth. And, again as we have noted, it will not flow unless there is a complete circuit. Think of it rather like a railway. If there has been a bad bit of points setting, the train which should have reached your station has instead been diverted on to a different line. That's a short circuit. If, on the other hand, a bridge has collapsed your train has not arrived because it is standing on the other side of the gap and can't come any further. That's an open circuit.

Of course, there's the third possibility that the train has been cancelled and isn't running. That is equivalent to there being no electricity at all. The simplest way to check that is to see whether any of the lights at all operate. If all bulbs are "dead," with the engine running, you have a major electrical failure on your hands. It is more likely, though, that you will find that some light and others don't, arguing a faulty circuit. Having decided what you are looking for you can proceed with your check. It will be much easier if you are carrying with you a simple test rig—a length of wire connected to a bulb holder at one end, with a darning needle soldered to the inner core at the other. You should also carry a long length of cable equipped with crocodile clips at each end.

Using your wiring diagram as a guide, trace the circuit backwards from the faulty component towards the source of power. If you find the wiring diagram depressingly like a small-scale plan of Hampton Court maze, try tracing out the one circuit you want with a pencil, remembering that what the diagram doesn't show is the earth return which makes up the second half of the circuit.

Work back along the lead, examining it for signs of broken insulation which could result in a "short." An open circuit, caused by a break in the wire core which may not have fractured the insulation, is more difficult to trace. Here, the bulb holder rig is useful. Earth the holder, switch on the current, and press the needle through the insulation at intervals along the wire. Don't thrust it right through. It need penetrate only enough to touch the inner wire. If the wire is "dead" your test bulb will not light. When the wire is "live" it will. When you come off a "dead" area on to a "live" one you have localized the area of breakage, and you need only probe a little more to find the exact spot. The insulation can then be cut, the inner wire joined, and the joint wrapped with insulating tape.

At a pinch, you can by-pass a whole section of wiring by connecting your jumper lead—that's the one with the crocodile clips—direct from the

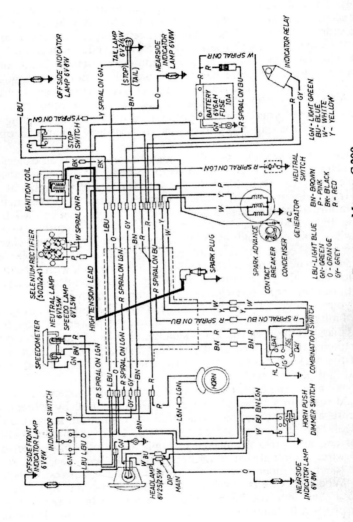

FIG. 9. WIRING DIAGRAM, MODEL C.200

24

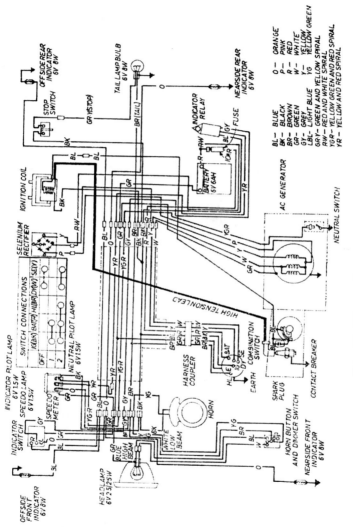

FIG. 10. WIRING DIAGRAM, MODEL S.90

25

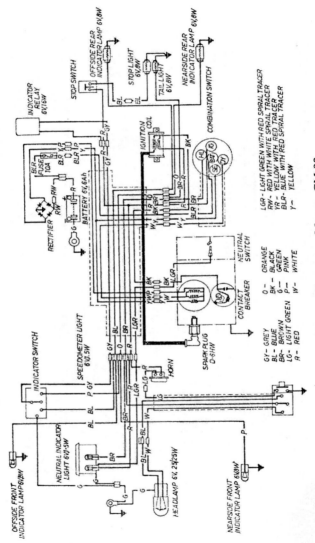

Fig. 11. Wiring Diagram, Model CM.90

26

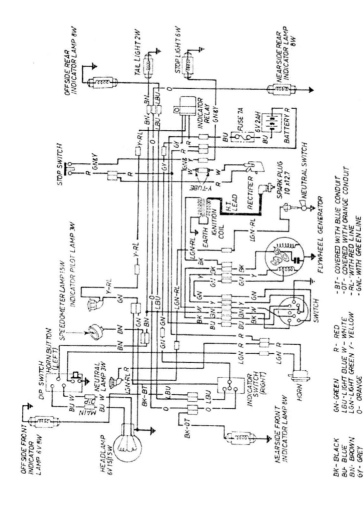

FIG. 12. WIRING DIAGRAM, MODEL S.65

BK- BLACK GN-GREEN   R- RED W- WHITE   - BT- COVERED WITH BLUE CONDUIT
BU- BLUE   LBU-LIGHT BLUE   - OT- COVERED WITH ORANGE CONDUIT
BN- BROWN LGN-LIGHT GREEN Y- YELLOW   - RL- WITH RED LINE
GY- GREY   O- ORANGE   - GNL- WITH GREEN LINE

27

power source to the component which you want to use. You will still have to trace and rectify the fault later on, but at least it can be done in the comfort of your own garage. Here, too, any temporary wire repairs which you have carried out can be made permanent. Rather than leaving a fractured wire twisted and taped together, it should have a snap connector soldered or crimped into place, together with a proper insulating sleeve.

You may, of course, find that loose terminals are responsible for either loss of contact altogether or for an intermittent contact. If this is so, clean them thoroughly and in the case of snap connectors tighten them by judiciously-applied pressure with a pair of pliers.

When making electrical repairs at home, remember that as a general rule a soldered joint is always to be preferred. The only exception here is if a bared wire is to be locked into a terminal by means of a grub screw, when binding the ends with solder may result in the screw working loose and making the joint insecure. Here, the screw should be well locked down so that it crushes the wire strands hard against the terminal, and so ensures good electrical contact.

5 Methodical maintenance

JUST as in everyday life it is more important to keep fit than to be forever taking medicine, so with your Honda you should aim to keep it in good running order by constant attention to its everyday needs, and not let faults develop to the point where components need to be stripped and rebuilt.

Now this may seem obvious enough, on the face of it, yet there are far too many owners who do just the opposite. Their machines are constantly in pieces; yet small defects, neglected, are allowed to become major ones calling for a fresh stripdown to rectify the damage. The strip-down in turn disturbs parts which had already bedded in, and the efficiency of the entire machine suffers as a result.

Given the specified regular maintenance, any of the Honda models can cover quite a surprising mileage before there is any real need to strip the power unit or even—thanks to its own efficiency and to the additives in modern oils and fuels—to lift the head for a decoke. But if routine maintenance is neglected the time which can elapse between overhauls is shortened drastically—and so, too, is the life of the machine. To make matters worse the overhaul, when it comes, has to be more extensive (and more expensive) as a result.

The reason is simple—maladjustments have a cumulative effect. The Honda engines are tough—remarkably tough—but they are as much pieces of precision engineering as any watch. Like a top-quality watch, the Honda depends upon its precision for its performance, and faults which are allowed to develop will naturally throw it out of its stride. Take, for instance, a tight tappet. This will cause little enough harm if it is rectified within, say, fifty miles. But in the absence of a routine check on tappet settings it could be left uncorrected for hundreds or even thousands of miles. Then all sorts of trouble can result from this one minor case of neglect. Searing hot gases from the combustion chamber— they reach temperatures of over 600°F—can play on the seating of the valve and on the valve stem like a blowtorch. Tough though they are, they will not withstand this treatment indefinitely, and eventually some of the metal is burned away. That leaves deep pits which, in turn, cut the compression still further, making the speed and acceleration drop off while fuel consumption rises. The entire engine is made to work harder to overcome this deficiency, wear is increased, and the life of such components as the piston and the big-end and small-end bearings is reduced.

Eventually, the least work which will make good the damage is to lift the head, recut the seat, and fit a new valve. Even assuming that there are no long-term ill effects, that's a pretty high price to pay for the couple of minutes saved by neglecting a weekly tappet check.

It is not, of course, only engines that can suffer in this way. The brakes are an equally glaring example. The linings wear slowly but constantly. The rider consequently gets used to their decreasing power, until the day arrives when he needs to stop in a hurry. Then he finds to his horror that they are not what they used to be, and he learns a hard lesson the dangerous way. Again, a constant routine check on brake adjustment—it takes a couple of minutes—will ensure that such a situation never arises.

Or, take the transmission. Out of sight inside its case, the chain is easily overlooked. Yet it has a big job to do and, inevitably, it wears. If it is not adjusted, there is a danger that under certain conditions it could even jump off the sprocket and jam the rear wheel. And it will certainly damage the sprocket if it is allowed to run slack, because the power is then applied at the ends of the teeth, which eventually become hook-shaped. When that happens the sprocket and the chain both have to be replaced, because a hooked sprocket will ruin a new chain within a few hundred miles.

Normally, it is recommended that checks should be carried out on specified components at intervals of so many hundreds or thousands of miles. Providing you keep a detailed log book this is as good a way as any—but how many of us do? Can you say for certain at what mileage you last tensioned the chain? Or took up slack in the brakes? Or did any of the numerous jobs which the machine demands? I couldn't—not on that basis.

But, then, I use a different method—based on the Task Systems which were employed to keep military vehicles in order. These set out tasks to be done each day, so that within a set period every essential job on the vehicle had been done and every vital point checked. For your Honda, which does not—I hope—lead as hard a life as the average Service vehicle, the routine involved need not be exacting. One can work either to a daily or to a weekly system, depending on the machine's utilization. If it is in use every day the daily system, of course, is the more appropriate. Where it is used mainly at weekends the weekly system will prove adequate. Carrying out the recommended checks should involve, at worst, no more than 10 minutes work each day and in most cases only a couple of minutes will be needed, for the idea is simply to check whether or not anything needs to be done. If the adjustment is already correct there is no need to touch it.

DAILY TASK SYSTEM

Sunday. Check adjustment of front and rear brakes. Check freedom of action of brake controls. Check security of all nuts and bolts in the braking system. Check lubrication of the brake cables and linkages.

Monday. Check engine/gearbox oil level. Check final drive chain tension.

Tuesday. Examine all exposed electrical wiring for abrasion or fracture. Test terminals for tightness. Test all lamps and switchgear. Check battery electrolyte level.

Wednesday. Examine tyre treads and remove any trapped stones. Check tyre pressures. Check spokes for security. Rock wheels and fork to check wheel, head and pivot bearings.

Thursday. Check clutch adjustment on motor-cycles. Check that automatic clutch frees on CM.90 scooter.

Friday. Test all nuts and bolts for security. Check operation of throttle and choke controls. Check fuel flow through pipe.

Saturday. Check tappet settings. Check sparking plug for gap and condition. Check contact-breaker points gap and condition.

ALTERNATIVE WEEKLY SYSTEM

Week 1. Check engine/gearbox oil levels. Check tappet settings. Check sparking-plug gap and plug conditions. Check contact-breaker for gap and condition of the points.

Week 2. Check the brakes for adjustment. Check all controls for freedom of action and for lubrication. Check wheels for loose spokes. Test play in wheel, pivot and head bearings. Examine tyre treads. Test tyre pressures. Check rear chain adjustment.

Week 3. Examine all electric wiring for fractures or abrasions. Test terminals for security. Check operation of lamps, horn and switchgear. Check battery electrolyte level.

Week 4. Test motor-cycle clutches for adjustment. Check that automatic clutch on CM.90 frees. Check fuel flow through pipe. Test all nuts and bolts for security.

Whichever of these two systems you adopt, you will be certain that all major points will be checked at least once every month. Even allowing for a pretty substantial utilization of your Honda, that means that no more than 300 miles is likely to elapse between checks—and that most defects will be noted and rectified before they have had any chance to develop into serious faults.

Neither system, of course, covers such points as oil changes and greasing. These must still be carried out on an elapsed-mileage basis, since lubricant is exhausted through utilization, not by mere time. But here again you can guard against essential work being overlooked by sticking a piece of coloured tape on the machine and noting on the tape the mileage at which the next oil change and the next thorough greasing has to be done. Fix this tape somewhere you are bound to see it—next to the filler cap on the scooter, for instance.

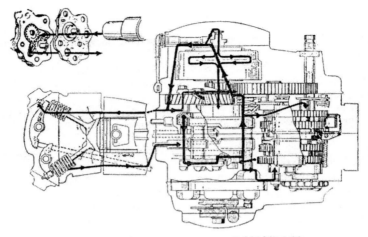

FIG. 13. OIL CIRCULATION, C.200/CM.90

The oil pump (*inset*) forces oil through the galleries indicated to lubricate the working parts. It then returns by gravity to the sump.

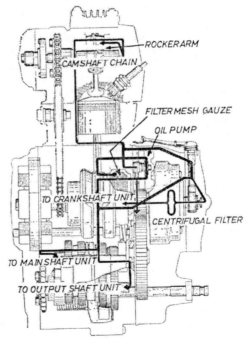

FIG. 14. OIL CIRCULATION, S.90

This is how the oil is circulated on the sports unit.

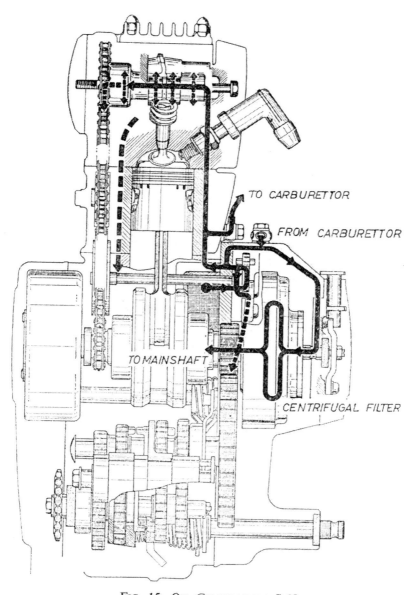

TO CARBURETTOR

FROM CARBURETTOR

TO MAINSHAFT

CENTRIFUGAL FILTER

FIG. 15. OIL CIRCULATION, S.65

On this machine, an external lead feeds warm oil over the carburettor mixing chamber to prevent icing.

It is a great mistake to overlook this periodic lubrication and, particularly, the oil changes. The Honda has only a small-capacity sump which serves both the engine and the gearbox, and the unit is very high-revving. That means the oil has got to be clean if it is to do its man-sized job. If the thin film of lubricant between the working surfaces were to break down the amount of wear which could occur in a very short time would be incredible.

Additionally, of course, the oil becomes contaminated in use. Tiny pieces of metal are rubbed off the piston and the bearings and the gears

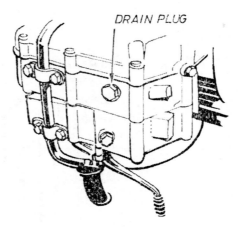

DRAIN PLUG

FIG. 16. SUMP DRAINING

On the S.65. this is the plug to remove when the oil is to be drained. Its sealing washer must be in good condition or leakage will result.

as they move. For every gallon of fuel burned in the combustion chamber rather more than a gallon of water is produced, and though most of this is expelled into the exhaust system with the gases, a proportion of it finds its way down the bore and into the sump. This is particularly so just after starting up, when the engine is cold and condensation occurs most readily. Once in the sump, the water mingles with the other products of combustion which manage to blow past the piston rings, and together they form sludge. Consequently, by the time the oil-change comes round that lubricant in the sump is no longer capable of doing its job properly.

It should be drained off when the engine is hot, so that it flows freely and carries with it as many impurities as possible. The drain plug should then be refitted and fresh oil of the correct grade used to replenish the sump. Don't use the wrong grade of oil. Before a grade is specified, technicians at the manufacturer's factory and in the laboratories of the oil companies carry out stringent tests to determine which is the best for any given unit. You cannot hope to better their choice; and in any case it is not worth risking a damaged engine or gearbox for the sake of saving a few pence on oil.

To ensure that the fresh oil is not contaminated with old oil, it is not at all a bad idea to give an intermediate flushing with a special flushing oil. This washes the oil passages clear. Then it is drained off—again, by removing both the oil filter cap and the drain plug, and the engine is allowed to stand for a quarter of an hour or so before the drain plug is replaced and the new lubricant poured in.

In all the engines dealt with in this book, the drain plug (Fig. 16) is located centrally, underneath the sump, and can be removed with a 17 mm spanner. Each of these models also has an oil filter and a gauge which need to be cleaned. The filter is of centrifugal design, in which sludge and metallic particles are separated from the lubricant by the force of rotation. Instructions for dealing with the cleaning of the filter and the oil-strainer gauze are given in the next chapter.

6 Looking after your Honda

ALL the routine jobs which need to be done on the 90 c.c. Hondas are basically simple and can, in fact, be carried out using the standard tool kit. Of the routine work, tappet, plug-gap and contact-breaker-points adjustment, taking up slack in the control cables, topping up the battery and adjusting the drive chain should be carried out as soon as the daily or weekly inspection shows the work to be necessary. Lubrication—including cleaning the oil filter—and attention to the air and fuel filters should be done on an elapsed-time or mileage basis.

TAPPET ADJUSTMENT

All Models. When adjusting the valve clearances—a job which must be done with the utmost precision if full performance is to be obtained—it is essential that the engine should be stone cold. It is thus better to make this the first job one morning, when the engine has stood overnight and before it has been started. If this is not possible, at least delay adjustment until the engine has had five hours in which to cool again.

Before starting the work, wipe away all dirt from the areas around the screwed rocker-box caps. If the engine is very dirty, wash the grime away with paraffin or grease solvent applied with a brush. Otherwise, a vigorous wipe with clean rag will suffice. The object is to prevent dirt entering the rocker box and so being circulated through the system with the lubricant.

The actual method of tappet adjustment does not vary significantly on any of the machines. Before work can begin, the timing cover has to be detached to give access to the timing marks on the generator and casing. The two screwed plugs on the rocker box are then removed to bare the rockers. Some riders—myself included—also prefer to detach the sparking plug so that the engine can be turned over more easily during the checking.

With all this done, turn the crankshaft so that the T-mark on the generator rotor is brought into line with the timing mark stamped on the crankcase. Then use a feeler gauge to check the adjustment of the valves (Fig. 17). If both have no play at all it is possible that you have selected T.D.C. on the exhaust stroke instead of, as is required, on the compression stroke. To check this, turn the crankshaft one complete rotation, so that the T-mark again comes to rest against the timing mark on the case. At least one of the valves should now have play, but if not there is a further method of ensuring that you have the right stroke. That is to watch the action of the valves as the shaft turns. If you have

T.D.C. on the exhaust stroke, the upper (inlet) valve will next be fully depressed by its rocker and will then close again as you pass B.D.C. at the beginning of the compression stroke. It is then only necessary to bring the two timing marks into line to be certain that the cams are properly positioned for tappet adjustment to begin.

The recommended tappet setting for all models is 0·05 mm (0·002-in.) but there are several schools of thought on this score. One is to give double this clearance on the exhaust valve, so that the actual settings become 0·002-in. inlet and 0·004-in. exhaust. On the other hand, some

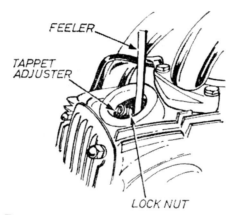

FIG. 17. CHECKING TAPPET CLEARANCES

With the engine set to T.D.C. on the compression stroke, the gap between the tappet and the valve stem must be checked with a 0·002–0·004 in. feeler gauge.

dealers with long experience of Hondas merely add a thousandth of an inch to both, to make the settings 0·003-in. My own preference is for the 0·002/0·004-in. method—but some riders prefer to stick to the standard clearances. However, though there is a certain amount of tolerance so far as a little extra play is concerned, there is none whatsoever for reduced clearances. The gap must under no circumstances be smaller than 0·002-in. or the valves and the performance will suffer.

To adjust the valves, place the 9-mm ring spanner (supplied with the tool kit) over the lock nut and fit the 3-mm "square" key over the end of the tappet adjuster, with a tommy bar through its hole. Release the lock nut by turning the spanner anti-clockwise, keeping the adjuster itself steady with the key (Fig. 18). When the lock nut has been loosened a little, insert the 2-thou. feeler between the valve and the adjuster. You should be able to slide it to and fro freely. Do so, moving it about an eighth of an inch back and forth, while with the other hand you slowly tighten the adjuster. You will suddenly feel the adjuster pinch the feeler.

Immediately, reverse the action and, keeping up pressure on the feeler, free the adjuster very slowly. As soon as you feel it release the gauge, stop turning, hold the key steady, and tighten the lock nut. You should now have an exact setting of 0·002-in., but as it is possible that the adjuster moved while being tightened you should recheck the gap. Obviously,

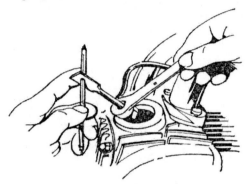

FIG. 18. TAPPET ADJUSTMENT

How to use the tappet lock-nut spanner, squared key and tommy bar from the standard Honda tool kit.

it will be no smaller than two thou. If it were, the feeler would be clamped hard between the adjuster and the valve. Therefore, it can only be correct or too big. Try inserting the next-largest feeler. If it will not fit, then your gap is correct.

Repeat the sequence on the exhaust valve, using the feeler appropriate to the gap you have chosen. Refit the caps, the plug and lead, and the timing cover and the job is done.

PLUGS AND POINTS

Checking the Sparking Plug Gap. Temperatures inside the combustion chamber of your Honda are considerably hotter than those in the oven in your kitchen. It may seem all the more incredible, then, that it is possible to maintain a set gap between two thin metal points under such conditions. In fact, it is not only possible but vital, for though the plug will work with a gap which is almost wildly incorrect the engine will not give of its best under such conditions. Regular checks on the gap are, therefore, one of the essentials of maintenance.

Such a check is easy to carry out. Detach the plug cap—it simply pulls off—and unscrew the plug from the head, using the box spanner which is supplied in the tool kit. On new machines you may find that the plug is a very tight fit indeed, and under these circumstances it is permissible to tap the tommy bar gently but sharply with a hammer to help free the plug. Be careful, though. Don't let the hammer slip and hit the cylinder or head, or it may fracture the cast-iron material. And don't let the spanner cant over, or the blow may fracture the porcelain insulator of the plug.

Make sure, as you take the plug out, that you do not lose the copper-asbestos washer which is sandwiched between the body of the plug and the head. This washer has two important jobs to do. First, it provides a gas-tight seal at the plug head joint. Secondly, it allows the nose of the plug to project into the combustion chamber by just the right amount. Without the washer, the nose would be too far in, and the build-up of carbon around the threads thus exposed could make the plug very difficult to remove at some later date.

Once the plug is out, use feeler gauges inserted into the gap to measure the clearance between the electrodes. This should be exactly 0·024-in., and if there is any significant variation the gap will have to be reset. But there is another factor to be taken into account, and that is the condition of the plug itself. It is useless setting the correct gap between two electrodes if one is burned away to a point and the other is severely pitted. So, unless the plug is obviously in good condition, I prefer to clean it first and square off the centre electrode with a fine file. When that has been done, I can see if it is worth bothering with that particular plug at all, or whether it would be better to fit a new one.

Cleaning the Plug. It is possible to clean the plug yourself, using a stiff bristled brush or a wire brush. In the latter case, however, try to confine your attentions to the metallic parts—the plug body, the side electrode and the central electrode. If the wire brush comes into contact with the insulator nose there is a danger of metallic traces being deposited on the nose, possibly leading to a high tension leakage. The better method is sand-blasting on a garage rig. However, if you do have this done, make certain that the garage gives the plug a thorough cleaning with compressed air afterwards so that all sand particles are blown out, otherwise these might fall into the bore.

The ideal is that the insulator nose, the plug body, and the faces of the two electrodes should be absolutely clean. The metal parts should be shiny. Don't forget that it is the underside of the side electrode which counts—the upper surface can be as brilliant as chromium plating, but if the side facing the centre electrode is black and pitted the plug will not be fully efficient. When you are satisfied by its condition, you can pass on to the actual gapping. If you are not satisfied, it is far, far better to fit a brand-new plug instead. They are cheap enough, and the extra efficiency is worth the slight cost involved.

Setting the Plug Gap. First of all, check the existing setting and note if it is too wide or too small. If it is wide, leave the correct feeler gauge in place and very gently tap the top of the side electrode, using the flat of a light spanner. Slide the gauge a little. It should move freely sideways, but not up and down. Try inserting the next-highest gauge. It should be too big to fit. If it is not, tap the electrode again and retest. Within a few tries, you should have the exact setting.

A gap which is too small must be opened up. This can be done by bending the electrode with a plug gapping tool, or by shifting it gently with the blade of an electrical screwdriver. In the former case, the tool is inserted from the side; in the latter, the screwdriver blade is eased in from the open end. Take great care not to touch the centre electrode as you do this, for it is esssential that it should not be bent. Keep checking the gap as already described, until it is exactly right. The plug can then be refitted to the head.

Fitting the Sparking Plug. This is one of those deceptively easy jobs which aren't as simple as they may appear on the surface. Before the plug is inserted, for example, it pays to smear a little oil or very light grease over its threads. This will make it easier to get it out again next time.

The sealing washer, too, must be in good order. The idea behind these washers is that they should not be fully flattened—just a little "spring" should remain to provide a gas-tight seal. If the existing washer has been crushed flat it will not make an efficient seal. Use a new one—you *can* purchase them separately without actually buying a new plug!

When offering the plug up to the head, be careful not to strike the electrode against any part of the engine. The reason is obvious—the blow could be enough to bend the electrode slightly and therefore alter that gap you have just set so carefully. And don't overtighten the plug. Giving a final wrench "just to make sure it's tight" may result in a warped plug body and a gas leak. The correct procedure is to insert the plug by turning the box spanner with your hand alone—no tommy bar—until it feels fully tightened. Then fit the tommy bar, and give the spanner half a turn to crush and tension the washer. And that should be sufficient.

Refit the plug cap after wiping away any dirt which may have accumulated inside it. And wipe the whole length of the plug lead too. Make sure that when the cap is fitted, no part of it is in contact with the cylinder head, since it has been known for H.T. current leakage to take place through the cap and being in contact with a mass of metal might accentuate this.

Checking the Contact-breaker Gap, Models C.200, CM. 90, S.90. All three machines use the same type of AC generator and the procedure for adjusting the contact-breaker points gap is similar in each case. Remove the timing cover, which is held by two screws, and turn the engine until the letter "F" stamped on the rotor is in line with the mark on the stator. The points will then be just about to open, and further movement of the crankshaft will bring them to maximum gap.

Before actually measuring the gap, check the condition of the points themselves. They should be grey in colour; and smooth on their faces. If they are rough and burned, they should be cleaned with a fine file before adjustment proceeds. If they have a yellowish tinge it suggests that oil is finding its way on to them, and the cause of this should be investigated. If they are bluish, it indicates surface burning and a faulty condenser, which should be renewed.

When you are satisfied with the condition of the points, insert a feeler and measure the gap. It should be 0·012-in., at the minimum and 0·016-in

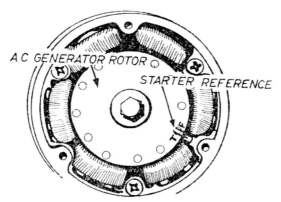

FIG. 19. THE AC GENERATOR

Used on all models except the S.65, the generator has timing marks stamped on the rotor and a reference mark on the stator plate.

at most (0·3–0·4 mm). Any variation from this means that adjustment is needed, since the gap has a marked effect on the ignition. If it is too small it results in the points staying closed too long, and this reduces the induction of H.T. current in the coil. If, on the other hand, the gap is too wide the duration of ignition is reduced and the efficiency at high speeds suffers.

Where adjustment proves necessary, loosen the two slotted screws which clamp the fixed point plate. Don't release them completely—only enough to enable you to move the plate, with a screwdriver, against their resistance. Insert a 0·012-in. feeler, and press the fixed point towards the contact on the breaker arm until the feeler is just free to slide between them. Then with a second screwdriver nip up the screws so that the setting is held.

Checking the Contact-breaker Gap, Model S.65. This machine has a flywheel magneto-generator, and although most of the foregoing applies with equal force the actual disposition of the components is somewhat different. To reach the magneto the entire side cover has first to be removed from the left of the engine. The mark "*F*" on top of the flywheel is then aligned with the mark stamped on the crankcase and from there the points are brought to maximum gap by inspection through the slot cut in the face of the flywheel. Measure the gap as already described, and adjust it by loosening the single screw which holds the fixed point plate, and inserting a screwdriver into the slot in front of the screw to manipulate the plate.

IGNITION TIMING

Adjusting the Timing, Models C.200, CM.90, S.90. Really accurate adjustment of the ignition timing demands the use of a special rig to show precisely when the points have broken, but satisfactory results can be obtained from the following method.

Working from the left-hand side, turn the engine over anti-clockwise

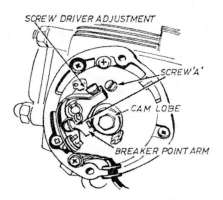

FIG. 20. THE S.90 CONTACT BREAKER

On the S.90, the contact breaker is mounted in the c linder head and is driven by the camshaft. Adjustment is by moving the fixed p int plate after loosening the screws marked "A."

until the "*F*" mark on the rotor has been brought into line with the fixed timing mark—the position at which the contact-breaker points are just on the point of opening. At this stage it is just possible to insert a 0·0015-in. feeler gauge. Should the line and pointer coincide with the points still closed your machine's timing is retarded. On the other hand, if the points are more than 0·0015-in. open it shows that they separated before the marks coincided, and that the timing is too far advanced.

To rectify either trouble is a fairly simple job. Two cross-headed screws hold the base plate. Loosen these, and turn the plate slowly until you obtain the correct opening between the points with the

rotor and static marks aligned. To rectify retarded ignition, the plate
must be turned to the right. To rectify over-advance, turn it to the

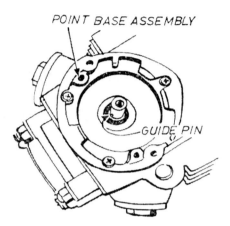

POINT BASE ASSEMBLY

GUIDE PIN

FIG. 21. POINTS BASE, S.90

The contact-breaker plate is fixed to this base, and the guide pin engages
with the cam.

left. When you have the proper setting lock the two anchoring screws,
and then recheck to make certain that the plate was not moved while the
screws were being tightened.

Model S.65. Only points adjustment is possible in the flywheel magneto
fitted to this machine, and any alteration of the ignition timing therefore
has to be made by varying the contact-breaker gap. You can set them
so that they are just opening (0·0015-in.) gap when the "*F*" mark on the
flywheel is aligned with the timing mark stamped on the crankcase. To do
so, proceed as for ordinary adjustment, but using the finer feeler.

CLUTCH ADJUSTMENT

Models C.200 and S.90. There is only one provision for adjustment on
the C.200 clutch, and that is to vary the relative strength of the outer
casing of the cable, by screwing in or out the knurled adjuster on the handlebar or the barrel adjuster on the cable itself (Fig. 22). Set these so
that the clutch-control lever has no more than three-quarters of an
inch play and no less than half an inch (actually, a range of 0·4-in. to
0·78-in or 10/20 mm). This is measured at the tip of the lever, and a
degree of movement within these limits should be obtained before the clutch
mechanism actually starts to operate. On the S.90, play must be only 0·4-in.

If less play is present, the clutch plates will be held slightly apart and slip and burning may result. If the play is more, the clutch may not free properly. To carry out the adjustment, loosen the knurled lock ring on the handlebar adjuster, and rack the adjuster outwards to take up excessive play or inwards to increase play. The actual degree of movement

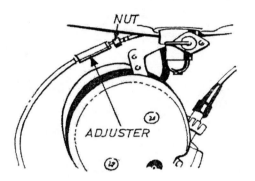

FIG. 22. CLUTCH-CABLE ADJUSTER

Both the S.90 and the S.65 have a barrel-type adjuster like this for altering play in the control cable.

can best be measured by aligning a rule between the tip of the lever and the handlebar with the tip at nought inches and noting the reading when the lever is moved to take up the slack in the cable. When the correct setting has been found, retighten the locking ring to hold it. When no adjustment is left, screw it fully home again and take up the unwanted slack on the barrel adjuster on the cables. (See S.65 clutch adjustment.)

Model CM.90. It is perhaps less easy to judge when the CM.90's automatic clutch requires adjustment, since there is no clutch lever to give one an immediate guide to the condition of the plates. Instead, it is a question of deciding from the actual behaviour of the scooter whether or not the time has come to make an adjustment. As long as the clutch engages smoothly when the throttle is operated and does not slip when you are climbing steep hills or carrying a heavy load the inference is that all is well. This can be double-checked by the lack of slip when kick-starting. Clutch drag, on the other hand, would be evidenced were the machine to jerk forwards when first gear was engaged from neutral— assuming, of course, that the tick-over had not been set too fast—and in a refusal to disengage when later gear changes were made.

As a general rule, if none of these symptoms are present it is better to leave well alone. When adjustment finally becomes necessary, it is quite asy to make it. In the centre of the clutch housing are an adjuster and

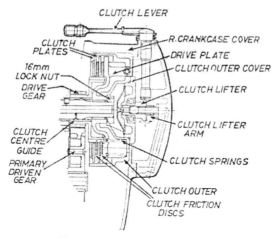

FIG. 23. THE C.200 CLUTCH

How the C.200's clutch is constructed.

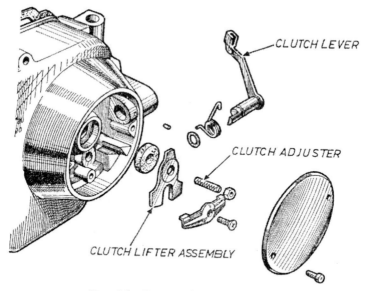

FIG. 24. CLUTCH CONTROL, S.65

The S.65 clutch operating arm and adjuster seen in exploded form, showing the clutch lifter.

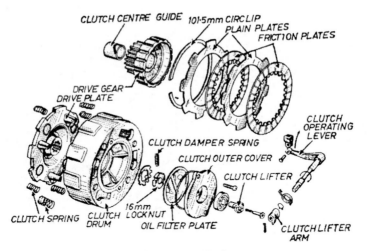

FIG. 25. THE S.90 CLUTCH

This exploded view of the clutch on the sports model clearly shows the relationship between the various parts.

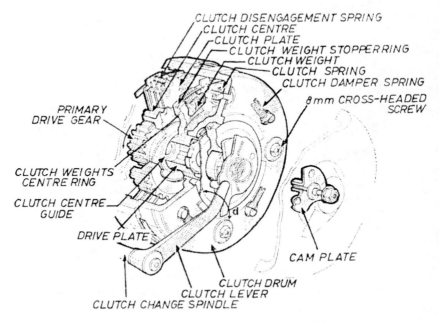

FIG. 26. AUTOMATIC CLUTCH, CM.90

As the engine is speeded up the clutch weights (*d*) move under centrifugal force and engage the clutch.

lock nut. The adjuster itself consists of a slotted screw controlling the
cam plate inside the clutch (Fig. 27). Hold the screw steady with a screwdriver inserted in its slot, and release the lock nut. There is no need to

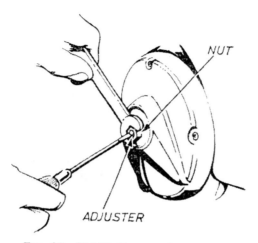

FIG. 27. CM.90 CLUTCH ADJUSTMENT

This slotted screw and lock nut are the sole means of adjusting the automatic
clutch. How to do the job is described in this chapter.

undo it—just free it by a couple of threads. Then turn the adjuster screw
anti-clockwise (to the left) very slowly until you feel pressure upon it.
As soon as you do, stop turning it anti-clockwise and give it one quarter
of a turn to the right instead. Hold it steady there, while you tighten
the lock nut, and your adjustment will be correct.

Model S.65. There are two forms of adjustment on the S.65—one on
the clutch cable, and one on the clutch centre. The cable adjustment is
made on a barrel-type adjuster situated alongside the main frame, just
behind the steering head lock. It has a lock nut, a hexagon-headed adjuster
screw, and a heaxgonal adjuster barrel. To use it, hold the barrel with one
spanner and free the lock nut with a second. The adjuster screw can then
be racked in or out until the correct free play (0·4–0·6-in. = 10/15 mm)
is obtained at the tip of the clutch control lever. This can be measured
with a ruler, as described in the C.200/S.90 section. When the correct
amount of play has been obtained, the lock nut is tightened on to the
adjuster barrel.

In practice, it is probably simpler to leave the cable adjuster alone and
so use the clutch-centre adjuster instead (Fig. 28). This is hidden below
the small plate set on the right-hand side of the engine and secured by

two screws. A slotted adjuster screw on the clutch-lifter plate has a lock nut which prevents it from turning. Free the lock nut a few threads first, and then use a screwdriver to set the adjuster itself. This should be turned clockwise to take up excessive play, anti-clockwise to give more

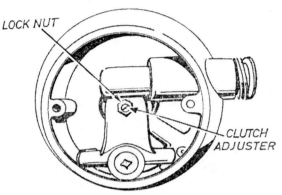

FIG. 28. S.65 CLUTCH ADJUSTMENT

To take up play loosen the lock nut and turn the adjuster screw. When the correct play has been obtained, retighten the lock nut.

play. When the correct setting has been obtained, hold the screw still with the screwdriver and lock the nut to hold the adjustment.

When all the range of adjustment here has been taken up, use the cable adjuster instead. When both are fully racked out, the clutch will be in need of new plates and a complete overhaul should be carried out.

THE OIL FILTER

Cleaning the Oil Filter, Model CM.90. On these machines, a centrifugal oil filter is built into the clutch drum. It should be cleaned after the first 3,000 miles, and thereafter at intervals of 4,000 miles. However, it is better to err on the side of caution, and attend to it more regularly than this—say at 2,000 mile intervals. Clean the filter after the oil has been drained but before refilling. To reach the filter on the CM.90 detach the cover of the air cleaner—held by a single nut and washer—and take off the front shield, which is secured by two bolts and a clamp on each side of the machine.

Detach the exhaust pipe and silencer as one complete unit, remove the footrests—held by four nuts to studs under the sump—and the kick-starter which is splined on to its shaft and locked by a nut and bolt.

The right-hand crankcase cover can then be detached by removing the ring of screws which secure it to the crankcase proper (Fig. 31). Inserted between the cam plate—fitted to the cover—and the clutch is a central spring. Be careful not to lose this as the cover comes away, and the cam plate and clutch lever are lifted off. In the centre of the clutch is a plate, which must be freed by releasing its screws. Beneath it is the

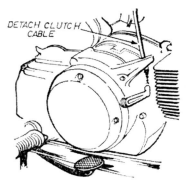

FIG. 29. THE OIL FILTER, 1

On the C.200 or S.90 start by releasing the clutch cable from the yoke on the operating arm.

oil-filter plate, which should also be detached. The interior of the filter can then be swilled out with petrol. Keep the machine canted to the

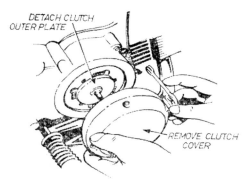

FIG. 30. THE OIL FILTER, 2

On the two-manual-clutch 90 c.c. machines, next detach the clutch cover and remove the clutch outer plate.

right when doing this, to ensure that neither petrol nor particles of dirt from the filter are able to enter the central hole in the crankcase. When the filter is clean, reassemble it and install the other components merely by reversing the stripping procedure.

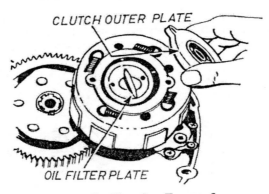

CLUTCH OUTER PLATE

OIL FILTER PLATE

FIG. 31. THE OIL FILTER, 3

On the CM.90 or S.65, in this illustration, the right-hand crankcase cover must be detached. Then the clutch outer plate should be taken off.

Cleaning the Oil Filter, Models C.200 and S.90. Owing to the lack of enclosure and the hand-controlled clutch, the C.200 filter is much easier to reach. Again, this should be cleaned at 2,000-mile intervals when the oil has been drained but before refilling.

Release the clutch cable from the yoke on the clutch-release arm (Fig. 29). This can be done by operating the clutch arm while holding the

REMOVE OIL FILTER PLATE

FIG. 32. THE OIL FILTER, 4

After detaching the clutch outer plate, take off the filter plate to gain access to the chamber. Note that on the C.200, shown here, only the clutch cover need be removed.

inner cable steady, and slipping the nipple out of the yoke. Then detach the clutch cover, which is held by four screws (Fig. 30). This bares the clutch face. Undo the screws which retain the clutch outer plate, beneath which is the oil filter plate (Fig. 32). Lift this out, and proceed as detailed for the CM.90.

Cleaning the Oil Filter, Model S.65. Detach the kickstarter pedal and the footrests, and free the clutch cable from the lever as described for the C.200. Then detach the right-hand crankcase cover to give access to the clutch. Subsequently, proceed as detailed for the C.200. There is also an oil-strainer gauze located in a housing just below the clutch. This should be pulled out and washed in petrol every 6,000 miles. Let it drain dry before refitting it.

Cleaning the Oil Strainer, Models C.200, CM.90 and S.90. These have an oil strainer fixed below the cover in the centre of which is the drain plug (Fig. 33). Every 6,000 miles this cover should be detached and the strainer withdrawn for cleaning. It is mounted in a metal holder. Wash it in petrol and allow it to drain before refitting.

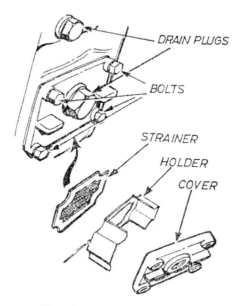

FIG. 33. THE OIL STRAINER

The oil strainer gauze is contained in a holder under the sump plate on CM.90 C.200 and S.90 models. It is reached by detaching the plate. On the S.65, removal of the right-hand crankcase cover is necessary.

LUBRICATION

Periodic Lubrication, all Models. Besides regular oil changes, there are lubrication schedules to be carried out on all machines. These involve such moving parts as the fork-link pivots (Figs. 34 and 35) and front-damper pivots at the front of the C.200, the CM.90 and S.65; and the

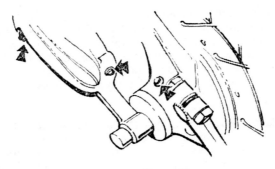

FIG. 34. FRONT FORK GREASING

Periodically give a shot of grease to each of these points on machines equipped with link-type front forks.

cables on all machines. The links are given a shot of grease through each nipple—there are four of them, plus a fifth on the brake plate for the speedo drive—once every 3,000 miles.

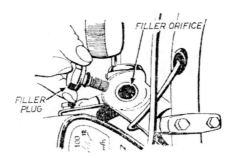

FIG. 35. FRONT FORK FILLER, S.90

Normally the S.90's forks should need no attention, but if an oil loss occurs the fork leg can be topped up by removal of this filler plug.

The cables are lubricated by being freed from their controls at the handlebar end, and having oil injected down the inner wire, using a pressure can. Be generous with the oil, since smooth-acting controls are vital and, in any case, you will also prolong the life of the cables. But a word of warning—under no circumstances must you oil the speedometer cable. If you do, it will act as a pump and inject the oil into the speedometer, which will then be damaged.

Besides these points, there are a number of others which will repay a spot of oil now and again. The best method is to start at the front and work backwards. So, first of all attend to the greasing of the suspension and oiling of the cables. Then give any exposed carburettor linkages a little oil. Lubricate the pivot of the footbrake, the anchorages of the return spring, the stop-lamp spring and the stand-return spring. The brake clevis should also be lightly oiled, as should the kickstarter pedal's pivot bolt and spring on the folding mechanism. Oil the clutch-operating lever pivot, too.

Don't oil rubber-bushed pivots—such as those on the rear dampers. Here, either use nothing at all or else apply a silicone spray. But don't overlook the drive chain. This works under good conditions in its case, but it will probably appreciate an annual lubrication. You can lightly oil the lower run through the inspection hole in the case, rotating the gear wheel so that the whole chain is covered.

On the S.90, with its open chain, this lubrication muct be more thorough, and the chain will have to be cleaned before lubricant is applied. Remove the chain by detaching the left-crankcase rear cover (held by three screws), and turn the wheel to bring the spring link into a handy position. Ease the horseshoe-shaped spring off by gently lifting one end out of its groove with a screwdriver and pressing the spring away from the link. The side plate can then be withdrawn, and the rest of the link pushed out to break the chain. Place it in a tray, and wash it thoroughly in petrol until it is absolutely clean. Then hang it up to drain dry, placing a folded newspaper underneath it to catch the drips, which will otherwise stain your garage floor.

When it is completely dry, test it for wear by extending it, on its side, and picking it up. Even a new chain, under this test, will take up an arc, but a worn chain will fall into a quarter-circle. If it has worn to that extent, it means that the chain and the sprockets should be renewed.

If you are to use it again, examine all the links for cracked or broken rollers and plates. If you find any, break the chain at the affected point by use of a chain tool—it is simply a clamp equipped with a screw plunger which presses out the rivet—and fit a new link.

I recommend using Linklyfe to lubricate the chain. This is a special graphited grease which comes in a large flat tin. Merely put a loop of wire through one link of the chain, roll the chain up, and place it on top of the lubricant. Set the entire tin on a gas ring or electric stove and allow the grease to melt. The chain will sink into it. Allow it to immerse itself completely, then remove the tin from the heat using plenty of thick rag to hold it—it will be hot! Lift out the chain and hang it over the tin to drain—and when it is dry you have a perfectly lubricated chain whose rollers are packed with grease. It is a clean and painless way of doing a normally rather messy job.

At intervals, you can keep up the good work by treating the chain while it is actually on the machine with brush-on Linklyfe—a special type which contains a solvent to make it suitable for brush application.

CARBURETTOR ADJUSTMENT

All Models. As a rule, little in the way of adjustment is either necessary or possible on the carburettors fitted to the Hondas. In fact, inexpert "tuning" is likely to do more harm than good. If an adjustment is made, therefore, make a careful note by how much it differs from standard, so that the original setting can be restored if need be.

Misfiring at intermediate speeds is an occasional complaint and it suggests an over-rich mixture. This may be due to a choked air filter, and this point should be checked before any attempt is made to cure it by adjusting the carburettor. The method is described elsewhere in this chapter. Once the air filter has been eliminated, the only other possibility is that the needle-jet setting is wrong or that the float-chamber fuel level is too high.

In the latter case, there will be misfiring all through the range and the carburettor will probably tend to drip fuel. If this is so, a professional check on the float mechanism is advisable, though experienced riders may be able to tackle resetting the level by judicious manipulation of the float arm.

The needle-jet setting, however, can easily be altered. Detach the mixing-chamber top and withdraw the throttle slide-needle assembly. Release the cable from the slide by compressing the return spring and easing the nipple out of its housing. Remove the needle-plate spring-clip, and the needle and its plate can be slipped out of the slide. You will observe that there are a number of notches on the needle, and that the plate is engaged in one of these. To weaken the mixture the needle needs to go further down the jet, and therefore the plate must be repositioned in a higher groove. Press it off the needle and refit it one groove higher up—i.e. away from the tapered end of the needle. Then replace it, fit the spring clip, pull the throttle cable out to its full extent and, holding the spring compressed as you do so, re-engage the nipple in the slot.

Had you wished, incidentally, to richen the mixture the procedure would have been identical, save that the needle plate would have been refitted in one of the lower slots, so raising the needle relative to the jet.

Before offering up the slide to the body, wipe it carefully with clean, non-fluffy rag. Then reinsert it, making sure that the slot in its side engages with the peg in the carburettor body before you attempt to press it home. This may call for a little judicious manipulation before you get it absolutely square, but don't be tempted to use force—you will only succeed in damaging the peg and, perhaps, jamming the slide solidly in the carburettor body. The net result of that would be the cost of a replacement carburettor—an expensive method of curing a slight fault in the mixture. When the slide engages, push it fully home and refit the mixing chamber top.

Idling Adjustment, all models. Although the exact layout may vary from carburettor to carburettor, the basic principle behind the adjustment for reliable slow running is the same in each case—to balance the degree of throttle opening (controlled by the throttle stop screw or the cable adjuster) against the strength of the mixture (controlled, in this instance, by the air-adjusting screw). On the CM.90, the former is the screw located on the left-hand side of the carburettor just forward of the float chamber

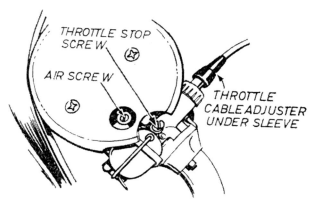

FIG. 36. THE S.90 SLOW-RUNNING ADJUSTMENT

The normal adjustment is by means of the air screw and the throttle stop screw. The cable adjuster is employed to remove excessive backlash from the throttle control.

bulge and the latter is on the same side, but higher up and to the rear, just above the bulge.

On the C.200 and S.65, the air screw is behind the vertical section of the mixing chamber and the throttle-stop screw in line with it, both on the left-hand side. On the S.90, the air screw and the throttle-stop screw are on the right (Figs. 36 and 37).

To make the adjustment, first of all let the engine warm up thoroughly. Then gently screw the air adjuster home so that it just comes to the end of its travel. Don't use any force at all on it. Having found its fully-home position, release it by one and a quarter turns. Start the engine, and manipulate the throttle-stop screw until a good tickover is obtained. Then try snapping the throttle open. The engine should pick up without hesitation. If there is a flat spot the mixture is probably over-rich, so release the air screw a quarter of a turn at a time until the throttle, when blipped, gives an immediate and clean pick-up.

This will have interfered with the tickover setting, and the throttle

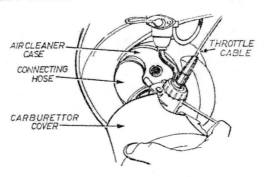

AIR CLEANER CASE

CONNECTING HOSE

CARBURETTOR COVER

THROTTLE CABLE

FIG. 37. ACCESS TO THE S.90 CARBURRETOR

To reach the carburettor on the S.90, release the screws holding the cover to the air cleaner.

will now probably have to be re-adjusted to slow the engine down again. In turn, this may call for one further slight adjustment—perhaps by an eighth of a turn—to the air screw.

Carburettor Cleaning, all models. In general, the carburettor is best left alone, since it is a pretty delicate instrument. From time to time, however, it does need to be cleaned, for dirt still enters the float chamber irrespective of the filtering system.

To clean the instrument, first wash down the outside with petrol to get rid of any road dirt. Then detach the mixing-chamber top and pull out the throttle slide and needle. Don't detach them from their cable. Simply tape them to the frame, where they will not be damaged.

Then remove the carburettor from the engine. Place it on a clean sheet of newspaper, and remove the float chamber by releasing its spring catch or, in the case of the CM.90, its screws. You will almost undoubtedly find dirt in the bottom of the chamber, and this should be swilled away with petrol.

Next detach the jets—only one at a time—and blow through them to make sure they are clear. If you find a blocked one which won't respond to blowing, poke it clear with a bristle. It is easier, incidentally, to clear a jet by blowing from the side opposite to that from which the air or fuel flows.

Replace each jet after cleaning, and when rebuilding the carburettor use new gaskets and washers throughout. This will help to ensure maximum efficiency.

THE AIR CLEANERS

All Models. The state of the air cleaner has a great deal to do with the overall efficiency of the motor-cycle or scooter. If it becomes blocked it acts as an obstruction in the intake system and will thereby cause a loss of performance, high fuel consumption and possibly misfiring too. To clear the filter element, detach it, tap it against a block of wood to free loose dirt, and then brush its surface gently. Some Honda experts suggest replacing the element every 5,000 miles—by no means a bad scheme, especially if it has already been cleaned once or twice during that period.

Models C.200 and S.65. On both these machines, the air cleaners are located behind a cover on the right-hand side of the machine and can be detached by undoing the single bolt which holds the element to the frame, the cover having been removed by undoing its knurled knob.

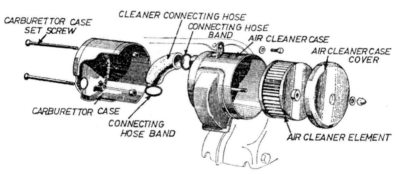

FIG. 38. THE S.90 CLEANER

How the air cleaner of the 90 c.c. o.h.c. Honda is constructed. The element must be removed periodically to maintain efficiency.

Model S.90. Here it is contained in a cylindrical housing in the curve of the main frame, just behind the engine, into which the carburettor projects. To remove the filter, undo the single domed nut on the left-hand side of the case and take off the cover. Undo the two cross-headed screws on the carburettor side, and detach the other cover-cum-casing. This gives access to the carburettor hose and retaining straps.

Pull out the filter element (Fig. 38) for cleaning or renewal. To re-assemble, offer up the element with the carburettor hose already in position, and the spring strap placed on the element stub. Engage the stub in the hose, slide the strap over it, and refit the two end covers.

Model CM.90. The scooter has a two-stage air filter (Figs. 39 and 40) —the sub-filter, mounted on top of the frame and containing one small element; and the air filter proper fixed below it.

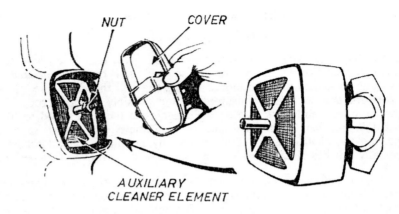

NUT

COVER

AUXILIARY
CLEANER ELEMENT

FIG. 39. CM.90's AUXILIARY AIR FILTER

Mounted on top of the frame, the auxiliary air filter has an element secured
by a single central screw.

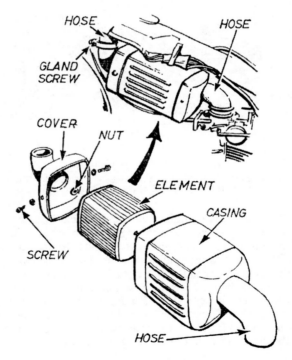

HOSE

HOSE

GLAND
SCREW

COVER

NUT

ELEMENT

CASING

SCREW

HOSE

FIG. 40. THE CM.90 MAIN AIR FILTER

This clearly illustrates the position and the construction of the main air
filter on the CM.90 scooter.

The sub-filter is reached by undoing its central domed nut and then the securing nut beneath it. The filter can then be withdrawn and tapped and brushed clean. To get to the main filter the front shields must be removed. The clamping screw on the top stub of the cleaner is then detached and the entire unit pulled off the carburettor hose. The top end of the cleaner is secured to the body by a pair of screws, and can be lifted off when these have been removed. Inside is the air-cleaner element, which is held by a single nut. Detach this and draw out the element. Clean it by tapping and brushing, or else renew it.

All Models. It is important to note that all Honda filters are of the dry type. Under no circumstances should they be wetted with oil; and any filter which is contaminated by oil or water should be renewed at once.

FUEL FILTERS

Models C.200, S.90 and S.65. In each case, the fuel filter is contained in a small chamber below the fuel tap. To clean it, switch off the petrol and undo the filter bowl by using a 10 mm ring spanner on the hexagon formed on the bottom of the bowl. A box spanner could also be employed, but don't use an open-ender—the metal is soft and the angles tend to get rounded. You may also have to support the tap body with a suitably-sized open-ender while undoing the bowl, which tends to stick. Don't use excessive force to free it.

When the bowl is off, lift out the synthetic-rubber sealing washer and the gauze filter screen. Wash the bowl in petrol—dribbling a little from the tap will be the easiest way—and the screen should be washed too, brushing away any dirt with a bristle brush. After that, refit them and carefully tighten the bowl so that a petrol-proof joint is obtained.

Model CM.90. In the case of the scooter, the job of cleaning the fuel filter is complicated by the fact that it is at the base of the carburettor, and this is therefore best tackled when the instrument is off the machine for routine cleaning, rather than by removing the carburettor specially for this purpose.

To remove the carburettor, take off the air-filter cover and the front shields, detach the air-cleaner hose and free the mixing-chamber top. Pull out the throttle-slide assembly and tape it to the frame.

The two fuel pipes will have to be detached, and as the tap is on the carburettor this means that fuel will pour out of them. Prevent this in one or another of these ways—either seal off the filler orifice in the tank; or insert plugs into each pipe as it is released, pinching it between your fingers to prevent fuel loss while this is being done; or pinch the pipe, detach it, and insert a length of plastic piping (about a foot long) into the open end. Keep the other end in the air, so that it is above the level of the fuel in the tank, while you pinch the second pipe and detach it. Then quickly press the free end of the plastic pipe into the remaining fuel lead and the two are effectively sealed off.

You can now detach the carburettor by undoing its two flange nuts. Underneath it, adjacent to the fuel tap, you will find a boss from which a bolt head extends. Undo this bolt, remove the cap and sealing ring, and take out the filter mesh. Clean it by washing it in petrol; swill out the filter housing and the float chamber; and reassemble in the reverse order.

THE SILENCER

All Models. There is no basic difference in the design and construction of the silencers fitted to the 90 c.c. Hondas, each of which has a tail pipe which should be detached for cleaning at regular intervals. The makers suggest every 3,000 miles. The tail pipe is secured by a single 8 mm bolt set at an angle on the rear flange of the silencer body, with its head facing the rear wheel. Undo and remove this and carefully grasp the tail pipe crossbar with a pair of pliers (Fig. 41). You can then withdraw it from the

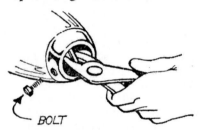

Fig. 41. Silencer Baffle Removal

After undoing the securing bolt, grasp the baffle end tube with a pair of pliers and pull it out for cleaning.

silencer body by giving it a sharp pull, twisting it from side to side to aid withdrawal if it tends to stick.

Clean it by tapping it on to newspaper placed over a block of wood, so shaking loose any soft deposits. Harder carbon can be removed with a scraper and a wire brush. The perforations or slots in the closed end must be completely clear. Finish off by washing the tail pipe in petrol.

It also pays to clean out the silencer body and the exhaust pipe from time to time—once every 12,000 miles or so. Detach the entire exhaust system; remove the tail pipe; and free the exhaust pipe from the silencer by loosening the clamp. Using a stiff brush of the type sold for cleaning gas boiler flues, brush away as much carbon as possible from the inside of the silencer body and, particularly, from its inlet pipe (Fig. 42). Tap the silencer against a block of wood periodically to jar out any carbon you have loosened.

The exhaust pipe may accumulate carbon near the bend. You can clean this by using a length of old cycle chain—any cycle shop will sell it to you for a song. The chain should be fed through the pipe and then see-sawed to cut away carbon deposits. That done, you can brush it through and reassemble the pipe to the silencer. Be careful, when inserting

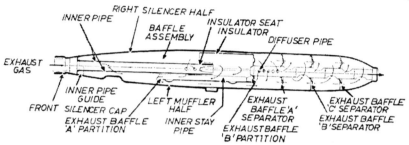

FIG. 42. A SILENCER IN CROSS-SECTION

Although only the diffuser pipe can be detached, the rest of the silencer's internals can be brushed out periodically to free it of soot and loose carbon.

it, not to damage the packing in the silencer inlet. Don't tighten the clamp at this stage. Offer the unit up to the machine and bolt both the silencer and the pipe into place first. That will allow a degree of flexibility and the two will be able to take up their natural positions relative to each other. Attach the silencer first, fitting it loosely so that it can pivot. Then attach the exhaust pipe to the flange on the cylinder. Tighten the nuts or the ring at the head first followed by the mounting of the silencer. Then lock up the clamp and, finally, refit the tail pipe.

BATTERY AND BULBS

Battery, All Models. Batteries require little care, but they demand it regularly. This is because, in use, the battery loses some of the water component in its electrolyte and this loss must be made good by adding distilled water to bring the level back to normal. Never use acid for topping up.

To do this, detach the battery from the machine—it is held by its clamp and the two electrical leads—and remove the cell plugs. With the battery standing on a level surface, add distilled water until the level of the electrolyte reaches the mark on the battery casing. You may find that a length of plastic tube is handy for this job. Dip one end into the water, place your finger over the other end, and water will be drawn into the tube. Keep your finger over the end while you insert the open part into the battery cell orifice, and then lift it off. This will release the water.

Another job that should be done is to clean the terminal posts and the terminals of the leads with emery cloth until they shine brightly. Then

before refitting the battery, smear them with Vaseline to prevent corrosion
It will not affect the electrical performance.

Light Bulbs, All Models. To reach the headlamp, speedometer, and
neutral-indicator bulbs, remove the front of the headlamp. This is held
by a recess-headed screw at the bottom. When this has been undone, the
lamp unit is eased clear of the bottom seating. The tab at the top then
disengages and the unit is free, save for the electrical leads. Free the bulb
holder and withdraw it. The lens unit can then be fully detached.

The contacts of the bulbs themselves and those in the holder should be
inspected at the start of the winter season and, if dull, should be lightly
polished with fine emery cloth until both are bright. This gives good
electrical contact. The same should be done at the rear, where the bulb
is reached by detaching the lens (held by set screws) and removing the
bulb by pressing it in gently and turning it. Where direction indicators
are fitted, the same procedure should be carried out. When refitting lens
units do not overtighten the fixing screws, or the plastic material may crack.

Stoplight Timing, All Models. In each case, the stoplight switch is
operated from the brake pedal through the medium of a spring. If the
lamp is slow in coming on—or does not light up at all—and the bulb is in

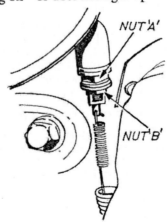

FIG. 43. STOP LAMP ADJUSTMENT

By loosening Nut "*A*" and tightening Nut "*B*" the switch body can be lifted, so
advancing lighting of the stop lamp. Reversing the sequence delays the lamp's
warning.

order it indicates that greater tension is required. Loosen the switch
lock-nut and raise the switch a little by screwing its top nut downwards
(Fig. 43). This advances operation of the stoplight. When it comes on

with the desired amount of pedal movement retighten the lower nut. To make it light up later, reverse this procedure.

CAMSHAFT AND DRIVE CHAINS

Camshaft Chain Tensioner, Model S.90. Unlike the S.65, which has a spring-loaded tensioner, the S.90's camshaft chain requires periodic

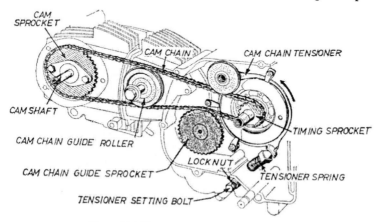

FIG. 44. THE S.90 CAMSHAFT DRIVE

On this machine, the chain is tensioned by the spring-loaded plunger, whose shaft is locked by a setting bolt. The guide sprocket also drives the oil pump.

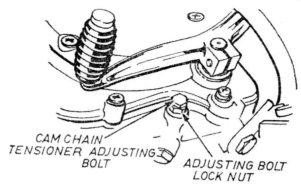

FIG. 45. THE S.90 CAM CHAIN TENSIONER

The cam chain tensioner bolt and lock nut on the S.90 are positioned on the left-hand side of the engine, as shown here.

adjustment. It is done by means of the adjuster bolt set low on the left of the engine, just forward of the gearchange lever spindle (Figs. 44 and 45).

Tensioning is a simple job. Merely set the engine running at 3,000 r.p.m.—about quarter throttle—free the adjuster-bolt lock nut, loosen the bolt, then retighten it. Finally, retighten the lock nut.

Drive Chain Adjustment, All Models. After 1,000–1,500 miles running, stretch and wear in the final drive chain will have caused it to loosen sufficiently to call for adjustment. In each case, this is done by drawbolts (Fig. 46).

On models with chain cases, detach the rubber plug from the inspection

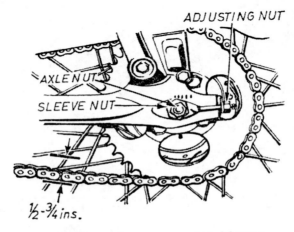

FIG. 46. CHAIN ADJUSTMENT, ALL MODELS

Only the S.90 has an open chain, but all Hondas use this form of chain adjustment. The stamped marks permit accurate lining-up of the rear wheel.

hole. Then loosen the rear axle nut and turn the drawbolt nuts one flat at a time to tension the chain. After both nuts have been moved by this amount, test the up and down play on the bottom run of the chain. The total movement must not be more than 0·8-in. and not less than 0·4-in. When the setting is right, retighten the axle nut, having first used the reference marks stamped on the fork and the drawbolt yokes to ensure that the wheel has been pulled back with the spindle square to the frame. This is important for if the spindle is set unevenly the rear wheel will be turned to one side, so interfering with the steering.

Where this does prove to be the case, the axle nut must be left loose and the settings of the drawbolts altered alternately until the marks on each side show the same setting. For example, if the marks indicated that the left-hand side of the spindle was further forward than the right, the left-hand drawbolt would have to be tightened and the right-hand drawbolt loosened. By this means, the correct alignment and the proper chain tension can be set. Always check the tension once more after the axle nut has been tightened, to make sure that it has not altered.

This adjustment should be carried out with the machine off the stand and with a rider aboard. With a little experience, however, it is possible to make the adjustment with the machine unladen and on its stand, and then to prop it against a wall, climb aboard, and lean down to check the tension with the left hand.

WHEELS AND BRAKES

Brake Adjustment, All Models. Screw-type adjusters are provided for brake adjustment on all models. Wear in the linings is taken up by turning the adjusters half a turn at a time, spinning the wheel by hand after each movement of the adjuster. Continue this until the brake is felt to bind when the wheel is spun. Then slacken off, half a turn at a time, until the wheel will rotate freely again.

It pays to check the brake efficiency regularly, by choosing a braking mark on a quiet stretch of road and making a weekly crash stop there from, say, 20 m.p.h. Note each time where the machine comes to rest, and when there is any significant lengthening of the braking distance re-adjust your brakes on the spot.

Wheel Removal, Models C.200, CM.90 and S.65. To detach the front wheel place a suitable wooden block under the crankcase to lift the wheel clear of the ground. Disconnect the brake adjuster nut and free the speedometer drive at the wheel end. Undo the torque arm or brake back plate nut. Detach the spindle nut and loosen the clamps. Then pull away the axle itself out of the hollow spindle to free the wheel. This comes away sufficiently to enable you to free the brake cable from its anchorage on the back plate, and the wheel is then completely free.

To take out the rear wheel, disconnect the rear brake-rod adjusting nut and remove the nut and spring clip which secure the brake anchor arm. Remove the spindle nut—the outer and smaller of the two on the chaincase side—and pull the spindle out. Next, ease away the tubular distance piece on the right of the wheel, between the brake and the fork. To detach the wheel, you now simply pull it to the right and drop it out.

Wheel Removal, Model S.90. To lift the front wheel clear of the ground place a wooden block under the crankcase. Detach the front brake cable and the speedometer cable—both at the wheel end—loosen the front spindle nut but do not remove it yet. Loosen the 8-mm nuts on the fork ends, and then remove the spindle nut and withdraw the spindle.

To detach the rear wheel, remove the silencer, and detach the nut and bolt which hold the rear torque arm to the brake back plate, so freeing the arm. Detach the rear brake adjuster nut, and disconnect the rod from the brake lever. Remove the spindle nut, the chain adjuster drawbolts and the distance piece, and pull the wheel to the right to free it.

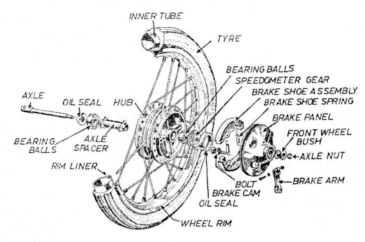

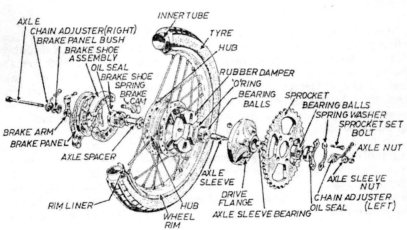

FIG. 47. FRONT AND REAR WHEELS

On all models, this is the basic layout of the wheels and brakes.

Fitting New Brake Shoes, All Models. Badly-worn brake shoes should be renewed as a matter of course. The best way is to use works-relined shoes.

The existing shoes are held in place by the pull of the two tension springs which are connected between the flanges of the shoes. These pull-off springs have a two-fold purpose. They return the shoes to the "neutral" position when the brake-operating lever is released; and they hold them in position on the cam and the pivot without chatter.

To remove the shoes, pull them outwards at the cam end, against the tension of the springs, until one end of each shoe can be freed from the cam and lifted up slightly. When this has been done with both shoes, rest them against the circular part of the cam to hold them, and repeat the exercise at the other end. The shoes can then be lifted away from the plate. That done, the springs are simply unhooked from the flanges.

Fit the springs to the new shoes, and offer them up as a pair. Pulling them apart, against spring tension, ease one end half on to the pivot. Then open up the other end, and ease that half on to the cam. It is then a simple job to press both ends down, so that one engages the pivot and the operating cam. Make sure that they seat properly and test the action of the brake lever before refitting the back plate to the wheel.

Spoke Tightening, All Models. Every 3,000 miles, check the tension of the spokes. Any that are loose should be re-tensioned by rotating the spoke nipple. An adjustable spanner may be used for this purpose.

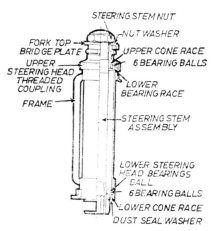

FIG. 48. THE STEERING HEAD

On all 90 c.c. and 65 c.c. Hondas, this is the steering-head layout employed. Adjustment is effected by screwing down the upper cone.

Steering Head Adjustment, All Models. The steering head should be checked for adjustment from time to time—once every 5,000 miles, say. Do this by blocking up under the crankcase until the front wheel is clear of the ground. Then grasp the front forks at the wheel spindle with one

hand and at the back of the top fork bridge with the other and try rocking
it backwards and forwards. There should be no perceptible movement.
If there is, it shows that the steering head bearings are loose and need
adjustment.

Where there is no play, make a second test. See if the front fork, when
gently displaced from its straight-ahead position, will fall freely from side

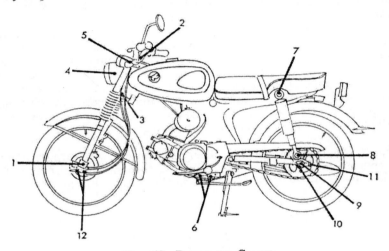

FIG. 49. POINTS TO CHECK

To ensure that your machine is always in top condition, check—

1. Spindle nut
2. Steering head nuts
3. Fork clamping bolts
4. Head lamp
5. Direction indicators
6. Footrest mountings
7. Upper spring mountings
8. Lower spring mountings
9. Rear spindle nut
10. Rear spindle sleeve nut
11. Drawbolt adjustment
12. Brake and speedo cables

On the other side ensure that the engine mounting bolts and the silencer bolts are tight.

to side. If so, the adjustment is correct and no work is needed. If not,
the bearings are tight and should be loosened.

To adjust, loosen the steering stem nut. Beneath the top bridge is a
slotted adjuster ring, which can be turned with a 36-mm C-spanner. In
the absence of such a spanner, it is possible to turn it by gently tapping
with a soft-metal drift and a hammer. Screwing the adjuster ring down
tightens the head bearings; releasing it loosens the bearing and makes for
freer fork movement. Therefore, if the initial test shows that there is
play in the head, the adjuster ring will have to be screwed down little by
little until this is eliminated. If the second test, on the contrary, shows
stiffness in the action the adjuster will have to be undone in easy stages

until the fork turns freely but has no fore-and-aft play. When this setting has been obtained, retighten the steering stem nut.

PERIODIC CHECKS

All Models. At least twice a year, start at the front of the machine and work through to the rear, testing the security of each nut and bolt (Fig. 50). Pay particular attention to any which have a direct bearing on the handling and braking of the machine, including the torque arm nuts and bolts and the domed nuts securing the rear spring/damper units.

At the same time, remove the various inspection panels and check that all visible electrical wiring is in good order and that no lead is being chafed against frame members, etc. Test the security of all the snap connectors and normally-concealed electrical terminals. All wires are colour-coded for easy identification, and reference to the wiring diagrams will tell you where any given wire should go.

Check the tyres thoroughly at thousand-mile intervals, setting the pressures and removing any embedded stones from the treads. If oil or petrol should get on a tyre, wash it off immediately with a strong detergent solution, since both are harmful to rubber. A tyre which is cracked around the casing, or which has cuts in the sidewalls, should be discarded at once. It is potentially dangerous.

Clean the machine regularly. Use a grease solvent to remove any oily or greasy deposits first, then wash the entire machine with cold water hosed on and sponged off. Dry it with a chamois leather, wrung out frequently in cold clean water, and then apply a wax polish. For this, follow the instructions given on the tin. It pays to leave a coating of pure wax on any surface which is vulnerable to water yet normally out of sight. This acts as a water seal and prevents rusting.

7 Pinpointing troubles

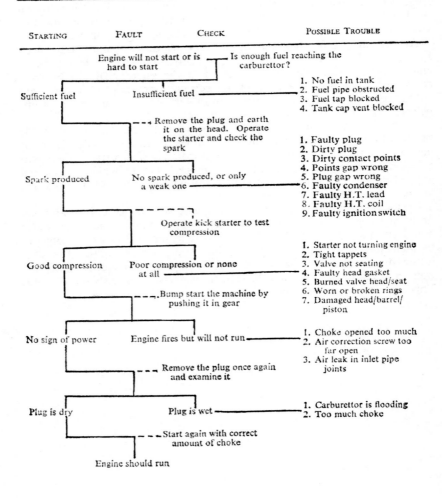

STARTING	FAULT	CHECK	POSSIBLE TROUBLE

Engine will not start or is hard to start — Is enough fuel reaching the carburettor?

Sufficient fuel

Insufficient fuel

1. No fuel in tank
2. Fuel pipe obstructed
3. Fuel tap blocked
4. Tank cap vent blocked

Remove the plug and earth it on the head. Operate the starter and check the spark

Spark produced

No spark produced, or only a weak one

1. Faulty plug
2. Dirty plug
3. Dirty contact points
4. Points gap wrong
5. Plug gap wrong
6. Faulty condenser
7. Faulty H.T. lead
8. Faulty H.T. coil
9. Faulty ignition switch

Operate kick starter to test compression

Good compression

Poor compression or none at all

1. Starter not turning engine
2. Tight tappets
3. Valve not seating
4. Faulty head gasket
5. Burned valve head/seat
6. Worn or broken rings
7. Damaged head/barrel/piston

Bump start the machine by pushing it in gear

No sign of power

Engine fires but will not run

1. Choke opened too much
2. Air correction screw too far open
3. Air leak in inlet pipe joints

Remove the plug once again and examine it

Plug is dry

Plug is wet

1. Carburettor is flooding
2. Too much choke

Start again with correct amount of choke

Engine should run

RUNNING	FAULT	CHECK	POSSIBLE TROUBLE

Lack of speed or pulling ------ Lift and spin both wheels
power

Both turn easily   Either does not turn easily
1. Brake is binding
2. Drive chain is too tight
3. Damaged wheel bearing
4. Hubs need greasing

- - - - - Check the tyres with a
pressure gauge

Tyre pressures are   Tyre pressures are wrong
correct
1. Punctured tyre
2. Faulty valve
3. Neglected maintenance

- - - Engage first gear, apply the
brakes and rev. the engine

Engine stalls   Engine still keeps running
1. Clutch is slipping—
adjustment wrong
2. Clutch plates are worn

- - - Slightly rev. the engine in
neutral

Engine speeds up   Engine does not speed up
1. Choke is closed
2. Air cleaner is clogged
3. Fuel line is clogged
4. Fuel cap vent blocked
5. Silencer is clogged
6. Main jet obstructed
7. Air leak in inlet pipe

- - - Test the machine on good
roads. Then check the
ignition timing and points
gap

Timing/gap correct   Timing/gap wrong
1. Defective adjustment

- - - Measure the tappet
clearances

Setting is right   Setting is wrong
1. Defective adjustment
2. Valve seat(s) in bad
condition

- - - Operate the kick starter and
test the compression

Good compression   No compression
1. Valve seat(s) in bad
condition
2. Rings and/or bore worn
3. Leaking gaskets
4. Valve timing incorrect

- - - Strip and examine the
carburettor

Carburettor is not dirty   Carburettor is dirty
1. Dirt is blocking jets

- - - Remove and examine the
sparking plug

Plug is clean and not   Plug is dirty or discoloured
discoloured
1. Plug not properly
cleaned
2. Plug is of the wrong grade

- - - Remove the oil filler cap and
check the oil level in the
sump

71

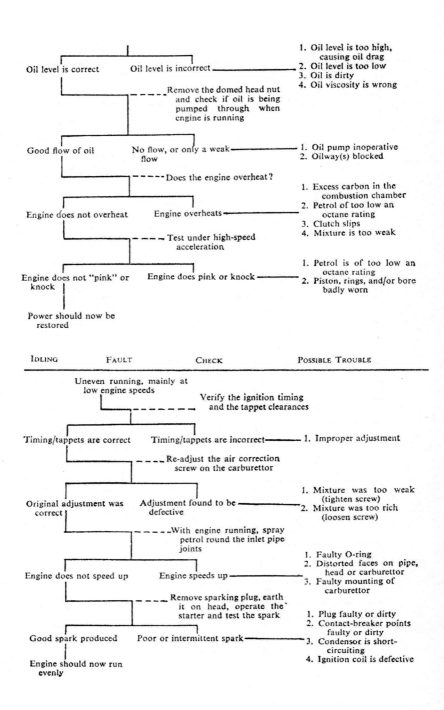

Oil level is correct | Oil level is incorrect ———
1. Oil level is too high, causing oil drag
2. Oil level is too low
3. Oil is dirty
4. Oil viscosity is wrong

– – – Remove the domed head nut and check if oil is being pumped through when engine is running

Good flow of oil | No flow, or only a weak flow ———
1. Oil pump inoperative
2. Oilway(s) blocked

– – – Does the engine overheat?

Engine does not overheat | Engine overheats ———
1. Excess carbon in the combustion chamber
2. Petrol of too low an octane rating
3. Clutch slips
4. Mixture is too weak

– – – Test under high-speed acceleration

Engine does not "pink" or knock | Engine does pink or knock ———
1. Petrol is of too low an octane rating
2. Piston, rings, and/or bore badly worn

Power should now be restored

| IDLING | FAULT | CHECK | POSSIBLE TROUBLE |

Uneven running, mainly at low engine speeds

– – – Verify the ignition timing and the tappet clearances

Timing/tappets are correct | Timing/tappets are incorrect ——— 1. Improper adjustment

– – – Re-adjust the air correction screw on the carburettor

Original adjustment was correct | Adjustment found to be defective ———
1. Mixture was too weak (tighten screw)
2. Mixture was too rich (loosen screw)

– – – With engine running, spray petrol round the inlet pipe joints

Engine does not speed up | Engine speeds up ———
1. Faulty O-ring
2. Distorted faces on pipe, head or carburettor
3. Faulty mounting of carburettor

– – – Remove sparking plug, earth it on head, operate the starter and test the spark

Good spark produced | Poor or intermittent spark ———
1. Plug faulty or dirty
2. Contact-breaker points faulty or dirty
3. Condensor is short-circuiting
4. Ignition coil is defective

Engine should now run evenly

72

MISFIRING	FAULT	CHECK	POSSIBLE TROUBLE

Uneven running at high engine speeds

Verify ignition timing and tappet clearances

Settings right

Settings wrong ——— 1. Adjustment incorrect

Disconnect the fuel pipe from the carburettor and test fuel flow

Normal flow

Weak flow ———
1. Insufficient fuel in tank
2. Fuel pipe is blocked
3. Fuel tank cap vent blocked
4. Fuel tap is clogged

Remove the carburettor and examine the jet(s)

Jet(s) clear

Jet(s) blocked ——— 1. Blockage

Fit a new main jet and test engine

Satisfactory running is obtained

Running uneven ———
1. Jet is too small
2. If trouble disappears with smaller jet either the air cleaner is fouled or the choke does not open fully

Replace the original main jet and check the valve timing

Timing correct

Timing is wrong ———
1. Timing marks not matched

Strip the head and test the valve springs

Spring(s) in order

Spring(s) broken, or weakened ——— 1. Spring(s) defective

Running should now be even

SMOKE	FAULT	CHECK	POSSIBLE CAUSE

Excessive smoke from the exhaust

Run at continuous high engine revs.

No smoke

Coloured smoke produced ———
1. Worn piston, rings, bore
2. Too much oil in sump
3. Rings fitted inverted
4. Damage to piston or bore
5. Metal fault in combustion chamber

Snap the throttle shut

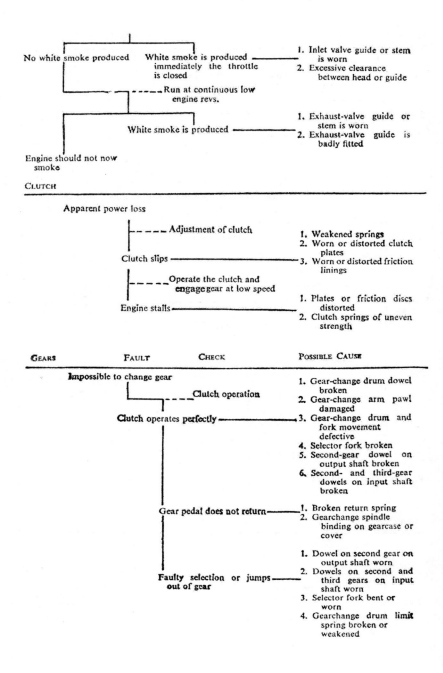

No white smoke produced

White smoke is produced immediately the throttle is closed
1. Inlet valve guide or stem is worn
2. Excessive clearance between head or guide

- - - - Run at continuous low engine revs.

White smoke is produced
1. Exhaust-valve guide or stem is worn
2. Exhaust-valve guide is badly fitted

Engine should not now smoke

CLUTCH

Apparent power loss

- - - - Adjustment of clutch

Clutch slips
1. Weakened springs
2. Worn or distorted clutch plates
3. Worn or distorted friction linings

- - - - Operate the clutch and engage gear at low speed

Engine stalls
1. Plates or friction discs distorted
2. Clutch springs of uneven strength

GEARS	FAULT	CHECK	POSSIBLE CAUSE

Impossible to change gear

- - - - Clutch operation

Clutch operates perfectly
1. Gear-change drum dowel broken
2. Gear-change arm pawl damaged
3. Gear-change drum and fork movement defective
4. Selector fork broken
5. Second-gear dowel on output shaft broken
6. Second- and third-gear dowels on input shaft broken

Gear pedal does not return
1. Broken return spring
2. Gearchange spindle binding on gearcase or cover

Faulty selection or jumps out of gear
1. Dowel on second gear on output shaft worn
2. Dowels on second and third gears on input shaft worn
3. Selector fork bent or worn
4. Gearchange drum limit spring broken or weakened

NOISES	FAULT	CHECK	POSSIBLE CAUSE
Tapping from region of cylinder head	Tappets		1. Excessive tappet clearance 2. Worn tappets
Metallic knock or ringing from cylinder	Internals		1. Worn piston, rings, bore 2. Worn small-end bearing 3. "Pinking," caused by excess carbon in the head
Rattle on o.h.c. machines	Cam chain		1. Tension wrongly set 2. Chain is stretched 3. Sprocket teeth worn
Rattle from clutch side of engine	Clutch		1. Clutch drum slots worn, allowing plates to move 2. Clutch loose on its splines
Rumble from engine	Crankshaft		1. Excessive end float 2. Worn or damaged main bearings

STEERING	FAULT	CHECK	POSSIBLE CAUSE
Machine tends to skid or pull either way		Tyre pressures	1. Too hard 2. Too soft 3. Not adjusted for pillion passenger
		Operation of handlebars	1. Head bearings too tight 2. Steering race balls damaged 3. Stem is bent
		Vibration from front or rear wheels	1. Wheel bearings worn 2. Bent wheel rims 3. Spokes loose 4. Rear fork pivot and/or bushing loose or worn 5. Frame is bent 6. Faulty tyre 7. Rear chain incorrectly adjusted
Machine tends to skid or to pull one side only			1. Unbalanced dampers 2. Wheels out of line 3. Front fork bent 4. Rear fork distorted 5. Front spindle bent 6. Loose head bearing

SPRINGING	FAULT	CHECK	POSSIBLE CAUSE
	Unsatisfactory operation of suspension	Tyre pressures	1. Too hard 2. Too soft 3. Not adjusted for pillion passenger
		Too hard	1. Front or rear damper not operating
		Too soft	1. Weakened spring 2. Load is too great
	Noisy operation		1. Friction between the fixed and moving parts of the damper casing 2. Friction between the casing and the spring 3. Rubber limit stop damaged 4. Hydraulic fluid level incorrect at front or rear

BRAKING	FAULT	CHECK	POSSIBLE CAUSE
	Brakes lack power	Adjustment at front and rear	1. Front brake cable binds 2. Brake rod is loose 3. Contact between shoe and drum defective 4. Water in the drums 5. Oil or grease on the linings
	No adjustment possible		1. Linings are worn 2. Operating cam worn 3. Shoe worn at point of contact with cam
	Noisy operation		1. Wear on linings 2. Dirt on the linings 3. Lining faces rough 4. Operating-arm bush worn

CHAIN	FAULT	CHECK	POSSIBLE CAUSE
	Chain needs frequent adjustment	Sprocket teeth	1. Wear on either or both sprockets 2. Teeth on either or both sprockets hooked 3. Wrong sprocket fitted
		Sprockets are serviceable	1. Adjustment neglected and chain has stretched 2. Periodic lubrication neglected

8 Overhauling your Honda

THERE are two main objectives behind doing your own maintenance work —unless, of course, you are already a keen amateur mechanic. One is to save time, the other to save money. Where there is no significant economy in either, I believe in letting the professionals take over.

In the case of the Honda, the saving is open to question, since a set of special tools is required. Whether or not it is worth buying these to tackle a job which you are likely to do only once during your ownership of the machine (if then, for Hondas are notably reliable) is very doubtful. On the other hand, you may cause damage if you attempt the work without them.

My advice, in cases such as this, is to carry out what I term a "peripheral overhaul"—to confine your own work to those parts which are readily accessible with the normal run of tools. Since this takes care of perhaps ninety per cent of the jobs likely to arise it is, to my mind, the most logical and economical method.

DECARBONIZING

A "decoke" is the commonest job of the lot—one which has quite wrongly acquired a reputation of being something of a panacea. "If the engine isn't running well, decoke it" perhaps sums up the general view.

It's the wrong view, too! You gain nothing by disturbing the engine unnecessarily. First of all, check *why* the engine isn't running well. Then, if it seems to be a likely cure, by all means carry out a decoke. But it is not a cure-all, and may even aggravate certain complaints, at least temporarily.

The object of a decoke nowadays, when fouling and carboning has been so notably reduced by oil and fuel additives, is to attend to the valves. On a four-stroke engine these are of the utmost importance, and they must be in good condition if the unit is to work well. If their seats are burned and pitted, their stems encrusted with carbon, or their springs weak, they cannot provide an effective gas seal and the engine cannot work at full efficiency.

For a decoke, you need the tools to remove the head and valves; a scraper; a small wire brush; a valve grinding tool; some fine grinding paste; a pint of petrol; a stiff brush; some grease solvent; and a few containers in which to place parts as you remove them. Begin by cleaning the outside of the engine thoroughly. Brush grease solvent all over it, working it well into the fins and paying particular attention to the under-side. Then gently hose it away, and dab the engine dry with rags. You can now start work.

Detach the carburettor and the exhaust pipe. Then remove the head. (The detailed instructions for doing this on the various models are given later in this chapter.) Hold the barrel steady with one hand while you bring the piston to T.D.C.

Using your scraper, remove any carbon from the piston crown. Many riders like a ring of carbon to be left round the piston, since this acts as an oil seal on older engines. The best way of ensuring this is to press an old piston ring against the top of the piston so that it just wedges in the barrel. Then use the scraper to cut the carbon up to the edge of the ring. Give a final clean-up with the small wire brush. You can, if you wish, polish the piston crown with metal polish too. This has no effect on performance, but it does make it harder for carbon to adhere to the surface, since a polished area offers less of a "key."

Now you can work on the head. Before removing the valves, scrape and wire-brush all the carbon out of the combustion chamber. Leaving the valves in place protects their seats from accidental scratching. Don't forget to pick any carbon out of the plug hole threads too. You can do that with a stout needle. When the faces of the head and valves are clean, you can finish them off with metal polish.

Next, remove the valves so that their seats can have attention. For this, you will need a valve spring compressor, though it is possible to "make do" by shaping a block of hardwood to fit inside the head and butt against the valves. With this placed on the bench, one can press on the valve collars and so free the collets. Detach the collars and the valve springs and remove the valves for inspection.

Before working on the valves themselves, finish off the head—now that the port is unobstructed—by cleaning out the exhaust section. Work from the pipe end, scraping and polishing until all carbon has been removed. Apart from the occasional attention to the exhaust pipe and silencer that is all the actual "decarbonizing" which needs to be done.

The valve seats and faces will need to be washed in petrol before grinding-in commences. It may even be necessary to take them both to a Honda agent for cutting. Pits up to 0·006/0·007-in. deep can be ground out. Any deeper than this will call for refacing. As it is difficult to measure the depth of a pit-mark accurately, the best bet is to reface if there is extensive pitting, or to grind in if there is not. If refacing is necessary, both the seats and the valves will have to be cut to an angle of 45 degrees.

To grind the valves in, smear grinding paste round the seating face of the valve and drop it back on to its seat—without the spring fitted, of course. Insert a broad-bladed screwdriver into the slot in the valve head and, pressing gently down, oscillate the screwdriver between your hands to turn the valve back and forth on its seating. After about a dozen strokes lift it up and turn it through 90 degrees—a quarter of a turn—and then drop it back and repeat the process. Carry on with this grinding until both valve and seat show an unbroken grey line of contact. Before you can see this, you will have to wash them in petrol. If the line is not complete dry them, smear on fresh grinding paste, and continue until you get the desired result. Then repeat the process with the second valve.

You can now replace the valves. Always use new valve springs after a top overhaul—springs weaken with use; and replacements are cheap. When the valves and springs have been refitted, test the efficiency of your valve seating by pouring into each port in turn enough petrol to cover the valve area to a depth of about half an inch. Then use a tyre pump to pressurize the petrol slightly. If none is driven through to the combustion-chamber side the seating is perfect. If petrol is able to pass through, however, so can gas—and the valve spring should be removed and the faulty seating ground yet again until a leak-free seal is obtained.

Rebuild the engine, and it should be good for at least another 10,000 miles before the work need be repeated.

DECARBONIZING—INDIVIDUAL MODELS

Head Removal, Models C.200 and CM.90. On the scooter, start by removing the front shield to give unobstructed access to the engine.

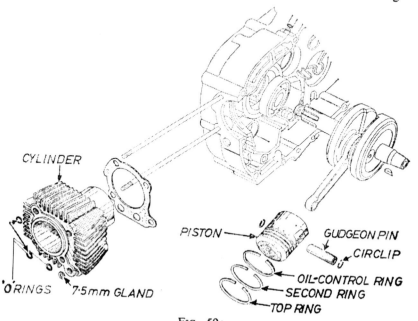

CYLINDER

PISTON

GUDGEON PIN

CIRCLIP

OIL-CONTROL RING

SECOND RING

TOP RING

'O'RINGS   7·5mm GLAND

Fig. 50A

Remove the air filter also. Thereafter, work is the same on both machines (*see* Figs. 50–52).

Detach the sparking plug cover and remove the plug. Remove the carburettor (and the inlet pipe, on the C.200). Undo the three head nuts

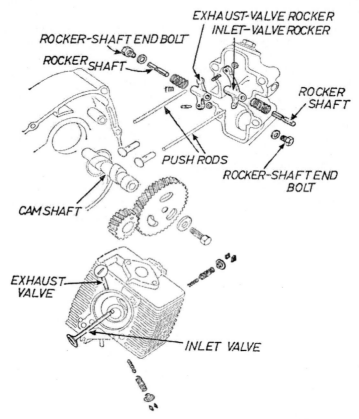

FIG. 50A AND B. THE CM.90 HEAD, BARREL, AND VALVE GEAR

The working parts of the CM.90 unit, shown here, are identical with those of the C.200

and the single domed nut on the rocker cover, and draw the cover off the studs. It may be necessary to tap the cover/head joint gently with a block of wood to break its seal.

Twist each push rod sharply to break the adhesion of the oil film in the cam followers, and pull out the rods. Then slide the head off its studs

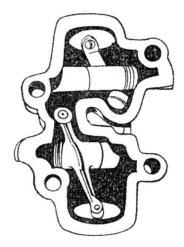

FIG. 51. VALVE ROCKERS, C.200/CM.90

On the o.h.v. models, the rockers come away with the rocker cover, and can only be detached if their spindles are removed first.

—again, tapping the head/barrel joint with a block of wood to break the seal if this proves necessary. In doing so, do not damage the head gasket or the O-rings used to seal the oilways. Replacing the head after the work has been done is a reversal of the removal procedure.

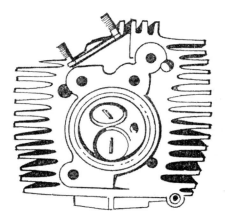

FIG. 52. THE COMBUSTION CHAMBER

This is an o.h.v. engine's combustion chamber, showing the slots in the valve heads used during grinding-in.

The tappets must be accurately set, following the instructions given in Chapter 7, and the clearances must be rechecked after the engine has been run for three hundred miles.

Note that when assembling, it is essential to ensure that the ball ends of the push rods engage properly in the rocker arms *before* the head nuts are retightened. The retightening should be done in the correct sequence, which is illustrated in Fig. 54.

Piston Removal, Models C.200 and CM.90. Should the oil consumption rise, it is possible that the rings need attention. This work involves removal of the head and barrel, and can therefore be combined with a decoke. Follow the instructions for stripping already given, but when the head is detached also slide the barrel off its studs. Support the piston as it emerges from the bottom of the bore, or it will fall against the studs and may be damaged.

The gudgeon pin is locked in place by circlips, one on each side. These fit into grooves in the piston and prevent the pin moving sideways. To detach a circlip, gently lever it from its seating by lifting its open end with a small screwdriver. When the end clears the groove, the clip can be levered outwards.

The gudgeon pin can now be pressed out, working from the other side. There is no need to detach the second circlip. If the pin is stiff, soak a piece of rag in hot water and wrap it around the piston. Within a couple of minutes this will have expanded the alloy sufficiently to enable the pin to be pressed out without undue force. The piston is then free.

Removing Rings. To detach the rings, gently ease them out of their grooves by expanding them. This is done by springing the open ends apart just enough to enable the ring to be lifted—but be careful, for rings are brittle and may easily snap. In fact, it is best to have a spare set handy just in case. When the rings are out, scrape any carbon off them (don't forget to deal with their inside surfaces, too) and clean out the grooves in the piston by using a piece of broken piston ring as a miniature scraper. Test the rings by inserting them, one at a time, into the top of the barrel and position them squarely about half an inch down. You can do this by pushing the piston in from the other end and using its crown as a guide on which to butt the ring. You can now measure the gap with feelers. It must be within the limits set out in the Appendix. Too wide a gap means that the ring must be discarded. If it is too small, open it out by gently filing the ends of the ring with a very fine file. When the gap is correct, wash the ring in petrol, place it on one side, and check the other two rings as well. New rings must be gapped like this before use.

Each of the rings has a different job to do and, therefore, each is of a different shape. The top ring is of square section with chamfered edges; the second ring is tapered, with its broader side at the bottom; and the third is an oil-control ring, which is recessed. It is essential that these should be fitted in their correct positions (*see* Fig. 53).

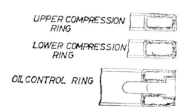

UPPER COMPRESSION RING

LOWER COMPRESSION RING

OIL CONTROL RING

FIG. 53. THE PISTON RINGS

This cross-section shows how the oil control ring differs from the compression rings.

Refitting Rings. To install a ring in its groove, it should be gently expanded by pressing its open ends apart with the thumbs. It is easiest to start with the bottom ring. Feed this up over the piston skirt, working from below, with the ends opened just enough to prevent them digging into the soft metal of the piston. Next, fit the middle ring—again inserting it from the bottom. Keep the oil-control ring compressed with your fingers as the middle ring is slipped over it. Lastly, add the top ring, which is easier to insert from the crown end of the piston.

In each case, it is essential to have the ring right side up. It is easy to recognize the top from the bottom, since the upper surface of each ring has stamped identification marks while the lower surface is plain.

Refitting the Piston. This is done, quite simply, by offering up the piston with the gudgeon pin inserted into one boss only, aligning it with the small end bush, and then pressing the pin home against the circlip in the other side. The second circlip is then fitted, using a new one as a matter of course.

Refitting the Barrel. Slide the barrel on to its studs, and turn the engine over to bring the piston towards it. Slip the end of the piston into the bore, holding the top ring compressed as you do so. As soon as this has entered cleanly, compress the second ring and slide the barrel over it. Then compress the third ring, and slip the barrel full home. The remainder of the reassembly is as already described (*see* Fig. 54).

Head Removal, Model S.90. Because of the position of the camshaft and the presence alongside the cylinder of the chain drive, decarbonizing an S.90 is more complicated business. First of all, the contact-breaker points cover on the left-hand side of the head must be removed, the leads to the contact-breaker disconnected, and the contact breaker detached.

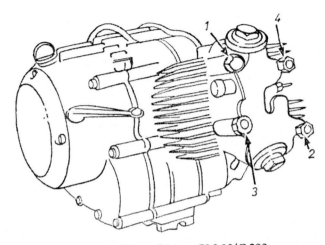

FIG. 54. HEAD NUTS, CM.90/C.200

On the o.h.v. models, follow this diagram when tightening the head nuts.
Take them up a few threads at a time to avoid distortion.

Then the 14-mm bolt set in the end of the camshaft must be detached and the centrifugal advance/retard mechanism withdrawn.

Rotate the engine until it is set at T.D.C. on the compression stroke, undo the two bolts which hold the camshaft to its sprocket, and detach the camshaft.

The cylinder head nuts can now be released, and the valve cover removed. Keeping up a constant pressure on the cam chain and sprocket (Fig. 55) which are still in the tunnel, ease the head off its studs. Have a piece of wire and a weight ready to attach to the chain, so that it will hang

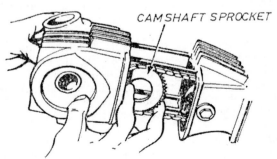

CAMSHAFT SPROCKET

FIG. 55. HEAD REMOVAL, S.90/S.65

When the cylinder head is detached from one of the o.h.c. machines, the camshaft drive chain must be kept tensioned with the fingers as shown here.

down and not jump off the sprocket teeth. If it should do so, the AC generator rotor and stator and the right-hand crankcase/gear-case cover will have to be removed to rectify it. They will, in any event, have to be removed if you wish to detach the cylinder for attention to the rings, since it is impossible to get the chain past the guide roller in the tunnel, and, therefore it has to be lifted off the timing sprocket on the main shaft

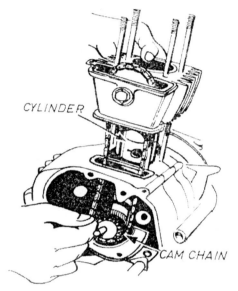

FIG. 56. S.90 CYLINDER REMOVAL

Before the S.90 cylinder can be detached from the engine, the generator must be removed and the cam chain feed from the sprocket as shown here.

and detached with the cylinder (Fig. 56). The work is straightforward, but time-consuming. Reassembly is in the reverse order.

To detach the valves for grinding it is necessary to remove the rockers. This is done by, first, removing the rocker side cover and withdrawing the rocker shafts (see Fig. 57). This frees the rockers, and the valves can then be removed in the normal way. On reassembly, note that the rocker shafts must be properly replaced (Fig. 58) with the shaft which has the small oil orifice in its end carrying the exhaust rocker. This orifice should be set away from the rocker cover plate, so it must be entered into the head first.

When rebuilding the S.90 unit the camshaft sprocket is placed in the chain and the two are threaded through the tunnel as the head is slipped into place. The piston must be set at T.D.C. for the timing to be obtained,

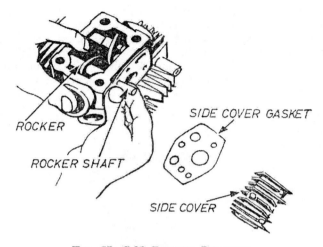

FIG. 57. S.90 ROCKER REMOVAL

To reach the valves on the S.90 (and the S.65) the side cover must be removed and the rocker shafts withdrawn. That frees the rockers, and exposes the valves and springs.

and the camshaft sprocket must be disengaged from the chain and turned until its marked teeth are in line with the mark stamped on the cylinder head. Hold it there and slip the camshaft into position, with its guide pin hole facing the top of the cylinder head. Then bolt it to the sprocket (*see* Figs. 59–61).

Use of a special oil-seal guide is recommended when fitting the points

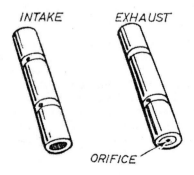

FIG. 58. ROCKER SHAFTS

On the S.90, the rocker shafts differ. They must always be refitted in their correct position or oil starvation may result.

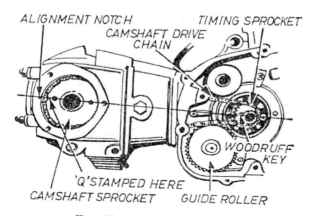

FIG. 59. S.90 VALVE TIMING

When retiming the S.90 engine, this is how the crankshaft and the camshaft must be set relative to one another.

base assembly, since there is otherwise a danger of the camshaft edge damaging the oil seal and causing leakage. Then the guide pin is replaced, the advance/retard mechanism is fitted, and the contact-breaker assembly replaced and wired up. Run the engine to enable the cam chain to be adjusted, and allow it to cool again before setting the tappets. Then adjust the ignition timing.

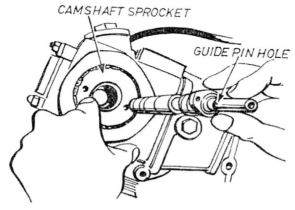

FIG. 60. S.90 CAMSHAFT REPLACEMENT

After decarbonizing, offer up the camshaft in this manner, keeping the chain tensioned all the time.

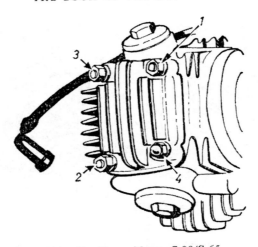

FIG. 61. HEAD NUTS, S.90/S.65

To avoid distortion, tighten the head nuts on o.h.c. engines in this sequence, taking each up a few turns at a time.

Setting the Ignition Timing, Model S.90. This job has to be done whenever the machine has been decarbonized, since removal of the contact-breaker unit will have interfered with the setting. The points cover and the generator cover must be detached and the crankshaft rotated until the contact-breaker arm is on the peak of the cam. The gap between the points is then adjusted to 0·012/0·015-in. by loosening the locking screw and turning the arm. When the gap is correct, lock the setting and then recheck it.

Now reset the timing by turning the engine until the generator rotor mark "*F*" is against the timing mark on the stator. The plate-locking screw on the contact-breaker base plate is then released, and the plate is turned until the points are just about to open. Then lock the plate with its screw and adjustment is complete.

Head Removal, Model S.65. Though the method of working on the S.65 is basically similar to that for the S.90, there are certain differences. The sequence is, first, to remove the two cylinder-head covers—first the right, then the left. Next, the engine is turned to set the camshaft to T.D.C. on the compression stroke and the sprocket is then removed. The rocker cover and head are detached, and the head lifted. To remove the cylinder, take out the cam-chain guide-roller's pivot pin, lift the roller away, and slide the barrel off its studs, feeding the chain carefully through the tunnel. Here, again, great care must be taken not to let the camshaft chain disengage from the teeth on the timing sprocket, otherwise the entire flywheel generator and the left-hand crankcase cover will have to be removed to give access for its replacement.

When rebuilding, set the crankshaft to T.D.C. and the camshaft sprocket O-mark right at the top—in each case, on both the S.65 and S.90, "*Top*" means pointing towards the front of the cylinder head—when refitting the chain.

Clutch Removal, C.200, S.90 and S.65. Remove the right-hand crankcase cover, detach the clutch lifter, and undo the clutch outer plate. Remove the oil-filter plate at the back of the filter chamber, and flatten the locking washer of the 16-mm clutch centre nut which is located behind it. With the use of a socket or box spanner the centre nut can now be undone. It is necessary to lock the clutch body during this operation. A special tool is used in workshops; but it should suffice if the machine is placed in first gear and a friend sits aboard and keeps the brakes applied while the nut is loosened.

To free the clutch plates, once the assembly is off, a compressor tool is used. This is fitted so that its central screw butts on the drive gear. You can use a cramp in place of this, with a wooden pad placed between the foot of the cramp and the clutch drum. When the springs have been compressed the retainer ring set in the groove inside the open end of the drum can be sprung out. Releasing the pressure will then permit the clutch plates and springs to be taken out. Rebuilding is a reversal of this work. Use a new tab washer under the centre nut.

Automatic Clutch, CM.90. The general layout of the CM.90's automatic clutch can be seen in Fig. 26. It is not advisable to attempt to dismantle it, so the private owner should content himself with merely carrying out the periodic routine adjustment already advised. If this fails to cure a clutch fault, the work of rectification should be entrusted to an authorized Honda dealer.

Removal of Generator, Models C.200, CM.90 and S.90. Except that on the S.90 the contact-breaker mechanism is mounted on the end of the camshaft and not on the crankcase, the method of removal is similar (*see* Fig. 62).

On the S.90, begin by detaching the left-hand crankcase cover. This entails detaching the gearchange pedal (held by a single bolt to its splined shaft) and freeing the cover screws. On the o.h.v. models, first remove the points cover and detach the L.T. lead from the contact-breaker assembly. Then remove the left-hand crankcase cover, and disconnect the lead from the neutral-indicator switch at the rear of the crankcase. On the S.90, it is above and behind the stator.

Undo the screws holding the stator plate to the crankcase, and lift it gently away, with its leads. Then undo the central bolt on the rotor, insert a rotor puller, and draw the rotor off the shaft. In doing so, be careful not to place too much load on the crankshaft, and do not lose the Woodruff key which locates the rotor.

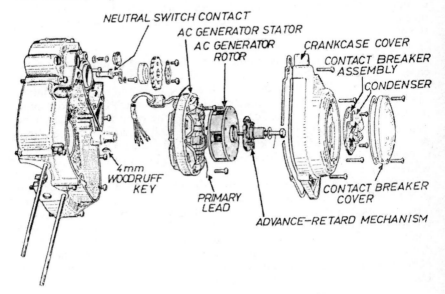

FIG. 62. GENERATOR LAYOUT, C.200

On the C.200 and CM.90, the generator and the contact breaker are both mounted in the right-hand crankcase, as shown here.

Refitting Generator, Models C.200, CM.90 and S.90. Wipe the rotor clean with a dry rag, and place its key into the slot in the shaft. Slide the rotor into place. On the o.h.v. models, fit the advance/retard mechanism and tighten the rotor bolt. On the o.h.c. machine, simply fit and tighten the bolt. Replace the stator and screw it into place. Reconnect the neutral indicator switch. On the C.200 and CM.90, refit the crankcase cover and connect up the primary lead to the contact-breaker. Then set the ignition timing, as already described, and refit the contact-breaker cover. On the S.90, simply refit the left-hand crankcase cover after connecting up the wires.

Generator Removal, Model S.65. Remove the gearchange pedal, held to its splined shaft by a single bolt, and take out the crankcase-cover screws on the left-hand side. With the flywheel firmly held—if you have no special holding tool engage gear (refitting the pedal loosely to enable first gear to be selected) and get an assistant to sit on the machine with the brakes on—remove the central flywheel nut and use a puller to detach the flywheel. The advance/retard mechanism is built into the inside of the flywheel itself, so be careful not to jar it.

Detach the wire from the neutral indicator switch, remove the stator-plate screws, and detach the stator plate complete with contact-breaker. Reassemble in the reverse order.

Contact-breaker Removal, All Models. The contact-breaker mechanism consists of a moving point carried on a fibre arm, which is spring-loaded to a terminal. To detach this arm, release the terminal bolt, taking very great care to note the order in which the washers are placed in relation to the terminal and the spring. It is essential that they should be refitted in the correct places. The arm itself is held to its post by a circlip. Press this out of the post groove and the moving arm can be detached. The plate carrying the fixed contact is held to the base plate by a screw. Remove this and the plate can be lifted off. Replacement is by the reverse sequence. When the points have been reinstalled their gap must be reset.

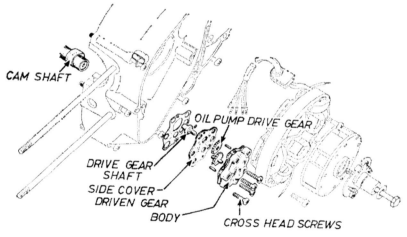

FIG. 63. OIL PUMP, C.200/CM.90
On the o.h.v. models the pump is located behind the generator, on the left of the engine.

Oil Pump, Models C.200 and CM.90. On the o.h.v. models, the oil pump (Fig. 63) is mounted in the left-hand side of the crankcase and is driven by a 2·5 mm × 10 mm pin on the end of the camshaft. It can be reached by removing the generator and it is then detached by removal of its holding screws.

Oil Pump, Models S.90 and S.65. On these machines, the oil pump
Figs. 64 and 65) is mounted on the right-hand crankcase and is driven

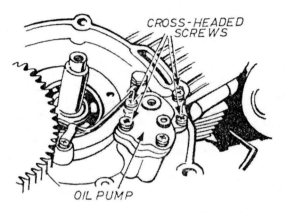

FIG. 64. THE S.90/S.65 OIL PUMP, 1

On o.h.c. models, access to the oil pump is gained by detaching the clutch.

by a cross shaft from the cam chain guide sprocket. To reach the pump,
the right-hand crankcase cover and the clutch must be removed. The

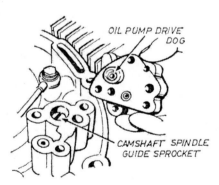

FIG. 65. THE S.90/S.65 OIL PUMP, 2

Removal of the screws enables the pump to be lifted off. Note the slot in the
driving spindle with which the dog on the pump engages.

pump is held by three cross-headed screws and can be pulled out when
these have been undone. To open up the pump, remove the remaining
two cross-headed screws. Installation is simply this procedure reversed.

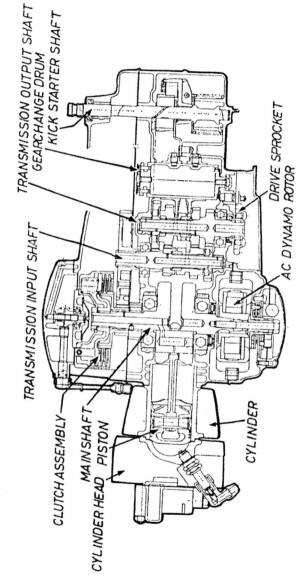

TRANSMISSION OUTPUT SHAFT
GEARCHANGE DRUM
KICK STARTER SHAFT

TRANSMISSION INPUT SHAFT

DRIVE SPROCKET

AC DYNAMO ROTOR

CLUTCH ASSEMBLY
MAINSHAFT
CYLINDER HEAD
PISTON

CYLINDER

FIG. 66. THE COMPONENT PARTS OF AN OVERHEAD VALVE ENGINE

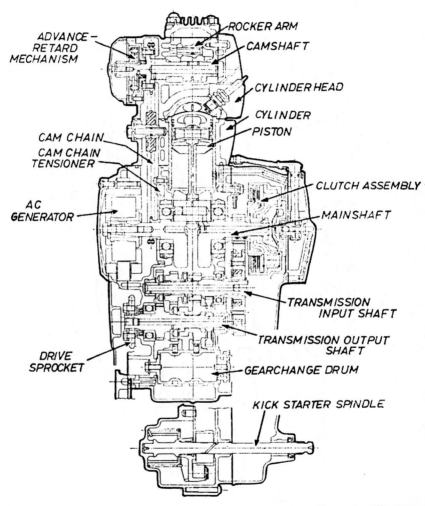

ADVANCE—
RETARD
MECHANISM

ROCKER ARM

CAMSHAFT

CYLINDER HEAD

CYLINDER

PISTON

CAM CHAIN

CAM CHAIN
TENSIONER

CLUTCH ASSEMBLY

AC
GENERATOR

MAINSHAFT

TRANSMISSION
INPUT SHAFT

TRANSMISSION OUTPUT
SHAFT

DRIVE
SPROCKET

GEARCHANGE DRUM

KICK STARTER SPINDLE

FIG. 67. THE COMPONENT PARTS OF AN OVERHEAD CAMSHAFT ENGINE

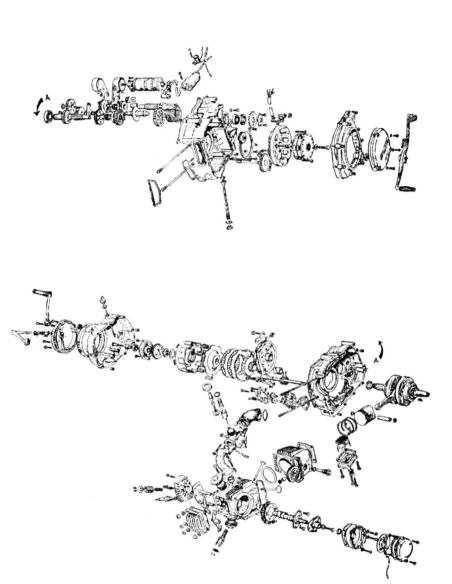

FIG. 68. THE S.90 ENGINE AND GEARBOX

Valve Timing, Models CM.90 and C.200. Provided the timing gears are properly meshed the valve timing must be correct. Both the timing gear on the main shaft and the camshaft drive gear have punch marks on their outer surfaces. These must be set adjacent to each other.

Engine Removal. To detach the engine from the machine, disconnect all the electrical leads at the snap connector on the main harness behind the motor and remove the battery. Remove the H.T. lead from the sparking plug and free the clip on top of the crankcase which secures the cable to the engine. At the rear of the unit, detach the light alloy chain cover and turn the rear wheel until the chain link appears. Then break the chain, connecting its two ends together with wire so that it will not fall into the chain case. Remove the air-inlet hose and, on the CM.90, the air filter. The front shields, of course, will have been detached before starting work.

On the C.200, release the clutch cable. Remove the carburettor and the inlet pipe (the throttle slide can be detached complete with its cable and taped to the frame). When doing this, be careful not to damage the inlet pipe O-ring. Next, detach the exhaust pipe at the cylinder head. Then remove the brake-pedal return spring from the rear engine-mounting bolt, take off the 8-mm nuts, and place wooden blocks under the crankcase to support the engine. Now take out, first, the rear engine support bolt and then the top bolt which supports the engine. The unit will then be free of the frame, and can be lifted on to the bench, and the footrests detached.

Engine Removal, S.90. The procedure is the same as for the Model C.200, save that there are three securing bolts instead of two—*see* Figs. 66–68.

Splitting the Crankcase and Gearcase. Special tools are required for this work, and for details of the equipment required and the procedure, reference should be made to the Workshop Manual for the particular model.

9 Fun from your Honda

SMALL though it may be, your Honda 90—or the S.65, come to that—is a go-anywhere machine which can be relied upon to take you on a long Continental holiday and bring you back again. It is one of the best, as well as one of the cheapest, methods of travelling ever devised.

Equip your Honda with a carrier—and with panniers, too, if you want to carry a bit of extra gear; fit a GB plate to the rear mudguard; fill the tank; and the roads of Europe are yours, from Dieppe to Dalmatia. Even the formalities are simple enough. You need a Green Card from your insurers to cover you for risks abroad; and if you are wise you will get the A.A. or R.A.C. to arrange ferries and other formalities for you and to provide you with your touring documents. You *can* manage without them, but since their services include shipping you and the machine back to Britain should anything go wrong the few extra pounds are well spent. The only other documents you need are a valid passport for yourself; visas for certain countries; and the written permission of the finance company to take the machine out of Britain if it is the subject of a hire purchase agreement.

As most motor-cycle insurance policies do not cover foreign touring you will probably have to pay an extra premium, and this can be extended to cover your riding kit and personal effects on request. Your insurers will want to know where you are going—and when—as well as the registration, engine, and frame numbers of your machine. You'll have to allow a few days for the cover to come through, so don't leave it until the last moment.

If you plan to camp—and it is easy enough to carry a small tent on the back of the bike, as many Continental riders do—you'll require a camping carnet, which will permit you to use sites maintained by any international camping clubs which are affiliated to British clubs. Sometimes it will earn you reduced fees, too. You can get it through a motoring organization or from a caravanning body.

Take your money in the form of travellers' cheques, with just a little in ready cash in the currencies of countries you propose to visit. And inquire, too, whether petrol concession coupons can be obtained. If so, these offer worthwhile savings on fuel.

Getting abroad is a pretty painless procedure for the Honda owner, at least financially. That twenty miles of water takes a bit of crossing as far as formality is concerned, but financially it's easy. The cost of a return air fare from Britain to France for machine and rider can be as little as £7, and the trip itself takes only 20 minutes. Allow 50 minutes all told, from arriving at the British terminal to riding away in France and you'll probably have over-estimated. The sea crossing alone, by contrast, takes 90 minutes, and since you will be part of a crowd of cars and people the formalities will take much longer than they do at the airports. On the other hand, the fare is likely to be a couple of pounds less.

As a touring mount, you can expect a Honda 90 to be capable of an average of around 30 m.p.h., quite comfortably, on Continental roads. Driving on the "wrong" side will cease to bother you after the first couple of miles, and you will find that it is possible to keep up higher averages than you would at home, while still seeing plenty of the countryside. So, if you put in eight hours riding a day you should be able to cover 250 miles—and perhaps a bit more—without tiring yourself. And that assumes that you leave the evenings completely free for exploration and enjoyment, and don't set off on the road again before 9 a.m. Were you a more Spartan type, in a real hurry, your mount would be quite capable of putting in an extra hundred miles each day.

What does that mean in terms of holiday grounds? Well, you could ride to Rome inside five days, spend five days there, and be home again easily enough within the confines of a fortnight's holiday. Given three weeks, you could reach Athens or the Black Sea and still have about a week in hand at your chosen destination. Or you could spend ten days on the Adriatic coast in Yugoslavia, and probably have time to do a spot of sight-seeing in the Austrian mountains on the way home. For a ride of a thousand miles in each direction, your transport costs—including flying each way over the Channel—would amount to a total of around £12. If you are camping, your accommodation costs would be low—perhaps £4—and as far as food goes it should cost you little more than it would if you stayed at home. Allow £30 all-in for a fortnight's holiday and you are unlikely to be far out, though obviously if you take all your meals in luxury hotels such a figure would hardly apply.

A pretty good guide to restaurants, at least in France, is to see where the "locals" go. Your Frenchman is a gourmet to his finger tips. Not for him the eternal British sausage, eggs and chips. He wants *coq au vin*—and gets it. And he doesn't pay through his nose for it, either. His haunts are marked by the distinctive "Routiers" sign. Make for it yourself if you feel that you cannot be bothered with cooking your own meals. Many camping sites, of course, have their own cafeterias, especially those in Eastern Europe. These are normally inexpensive.

In Italy, head for any *trattoria* which is obviously well frequented by the local folk. In Jugoslavia, keep an eye open for motels and for open-air cafés, where you can obtain a good *kebab* for a few shillings.

Alternatively, you may care to head for Scandinavia. One shipping company, operating from Newcastle, will actually carry your machine free of charge if you accompany it. Scandinavia in the summer is a wonderful touring ground—not too hot, and with long days and short nights. If you get near the Arctic Circle (quite warm at that time of year) you end up by having no night at all—just a quick dusk followed immediately by dawn.

Britain, of course, is one of the finest touring grounds in the world, save for its rather unpredictable climate. Given a couple of hundred miles motoring each day, you could virtually ride round the entire coastline in a fortnight's holiday. And the remoter parts of Scotland and Wales are ideal for a holiday "away from it all." Here, you can often ride for hours at a time without meeting another vehicle or, indeed, without seeing another person. You can also ride for long distances without seeing a filling station either, so be sure to carry a spare can of petrol with you.

Hondas and holidays, then, go together. But what about weekends? There are, obviously, plenty of opportunities for making weekend trips. Leaving sharp after work on Friday, one can put in well over a hundred miles in the evening, so a weekend in the New Forest is a distinct possibility for Londoners. But there is another aspect too—club life—which your Honda can open up for you. There are over 600 motor-cycle clubs in Britain, and at the cost of a small annual subscription you can join one of these and take part in its organized social and sporting events. These may range from weekend runs to non-frame-breaking trials for standard machines—and here your Honda will more than hold its own. Besides adding to your circle of friends you will find that club life broadens your outlook on motor-cycling and helps you to learn more about caring for and riding motor-cycles by bringing you into the company and confidence of other enthusiasts. You can obtain the address of the secretary of your local club, or of the Honda Owners' Club, from the A.-C.U., 83 Pall Mall, London, S.W.1.

Perhaps you feel that you would like to put your machine to some social use? In that case, you could join the Volunteer Emergency Service —an organization founded during a smallpox scare some years ago by two motor-cycling enthusiasts, Barry and Margaret Ryerson. Vaccines had to be distributed in a hurry, and the Ryersons realized that volunteer riders drawn from the clubs could do this faster than could any of the official services then existing. From that idea has grown the V.E.S.—a wonderful stand-by corps of riders willing to be on call in their spare time to help others. What a superb answer it is to the ill-informed criticism which so often besets motor-cyclists—and what a rewarding way of spending one's time. Further information on the V.E.S. can be obtained from its headquarters at 1 Plough Lane, Wallington, Surrey.

Whether for work or play, or for social service, I am sure you will find that your Honda 90 will give you the same pleasure that my own Hondas have done in the past. Repay your machine by looking after it in the way described in this book and it will never let you down. If, in these pages, I have been able to give you a little more insight into the way it works and in how to get the best out of it I am amply repaid, not least in the certainty that another fellow-motor-cyclist is enjoying trouble-free motor-cycling in one of the best ways that there is—on a well-tuned, sweet-running, hairline-steering Honda.

Facts and Figures

DATA	CM.90 o.h.v.	C.200	S 90	S.65
Bore . . .	49 mm	49 mm	50 mm	44 mm
Stroke . . .	46 mm	46 mm	45·6 mm	41·4 mm
Capacity . .	86·7 c.c.	86·7 c.c.	89·6 c.c.	63 c.c.
C.R. . .	8:1	8:1	8·2:1	8·8:1
Output . . .	7·5 b.h.p. at 7,500 r.p.m.	6·5 b.h.p. at 8,000 r.p.m.	8 b.h.p. at 9,500 r.p.m.	6·2 b.h.p. at 10,000 r.p.m.
Oil capacity . .	0·68 pints	0·68 pints	1½ pints	¾ pint
Oil grade (winter) .	S.A.E. 30	S.A.E. 30	S.A.E. 30	S.A.E. 30
(summer) .				
Fuel tank capacity	9 pints	1·9 gal.	1½ gal.	1·4 gal.
Sparking plug .	Type N.G.K. D–7–H	N.G.K. D–7–H	N.G.K. D–8–H or D–10–H	N.G.K. D–7–H
Tyre pressure (front) .	24 lb/sq in. (1·7 kg/sq cm)	24 lb/sq in. (1·7 kg/sq cm)	26 lb/sq in. (1·8 kg/sq cm)	24 lb/sq in. (1·7 kg/sq cm)
rear) .	30 lb/sq in. (2·1 kg/sq cm)	30 lb/sq in. (2·1 kg/sq cm)	32 lb/sq in. (2·2 kg/sq cm)	30 lb/sq in. (2·1 kg/sq cm)
Add for pillion .	4 lb/sq in. (0·3 kg/sq cm)	4 lb/sq in. (0·3 kg/sq cm)	4 lb/sq in. (0·3 kg/sq cm)	4 lb/sq in. (0·3 kg/sq cm)
Bulbs: headlamp .	6 v 25/25 w	6 v 25/25 w	6 v 25/25 w	6 v 15/15 w
tail . .	6 v 2 w	6 c 2 w	6 v 2 w	6 v 2 w
stop .	6 v 6 w	6 v 6 w	6 v 6 w	6 v 6 w
winker .	6 v 16 w	6 v 16 w	—	—
winker indicator	6 v 1·5 w	6 v 1·5 w	—	—
neutral .	6 v 1·5 w	6 v 1·5 w	6 v 1·5 w	6 v 1·5 w
speedo .	6 v 1·5 w	6 v 1·5 w	6 v 1·5 w	6 v 1·5 w
Weight (dry) .	183 lb	171 lb	190 lb	171 lb
Length . .	71 in.	72 in.	74 in.	69·2 in.
Width . . .	23 in.	25 in.	25½ in.	23·8 in.
Height . .	38 in.	38 in.	38¼ in.	33·4 in.
Ground clearance .	5 in.	5½ in.	4¼ in.	4·9 in.
Tyre sizes . .	2·50 × 17 in.	2·50 × 17 in.	2·50 × 18 in.	2·25 × 17 in.
Contact-breaker gap	0·012/15 in.	0·012/15 in.	0·012/15 in.	0·012/15 in.
Sparking-plug gap .	0·025 in.	0·025 in.	0·025 in.	0·025 in.
Tappet clearances . .	0·002/4 in.	0·002/4 in.	0·002 in.	0·002 in.
Ring gaps	0·004–0·012 in., all models			

Index

OTHER MOTORCYCLE MANUALS AVAILABLE IN THIS SERIES

ARIEL WORKSHOP MANUAL 1933-1951:
All single, twin & 4 cylinder models

ARIEL (BOOK OF) MAINTENANCE & REPAIR MANUAL 1932-1939:
LF3, LF4, LG, NF3, NF4, NG, OG, VA, VA3, VA4, VB, VF3, VF4, VG,
Red Hunter LH, NH, OH, VH & Square Four 4F, 4G, 4H

BMW FACTORY WORKSHOP MANUAL R27, R28:
English, German, French and Spanish text

BMW FACTORY WORKSHOP MANUAL R50, R50S, R60, R69S:
Also includes a supplement for the USA models: R50US, R60US, R69US.
English, German, French and Spanish text

BSA PRE-WAR SINGLES & TWINS (BOOK OF) 1936-1939:
All Pre-War single & twin cylinder SV & OHV models through 1939
150cc, 250cc, 350cc, 500cc, 600cc, 750cc & 1,000cc

BSA SINGLES (BOOK OF) 1945-1954:
OHV & SV 250cc, 350cc, 500cc & 600cc, Groups B, C & M

BSA SINGLES (BOOK OF) 1955-1967:
B31, B32, B33, B34 and "Star" B40 & SS90

BSA 250cc SINGLES (BOOK OF) 1954-1970:
B31, B32, B33, B34 and "Star" B40 & SS90

BSA TWINS (BOOK OF) 1948-1962:
All 650cc & 500cc twins

DUCATI OHC FACTORY WORKSHOP MANUAL:
160 Junior Monza, 250 Monza, 250 GT, 250 Mark 3, 250 Mach 1, 250 SCR &
350 Sebring

HONDA 250 & 305cc FACTORY WORKSHOP MANUAL:
C.72 C.77 CS.72, CS.77, CB.72, CB.77 [HAWK]

HONDA 125 & 150cc FACTORY WORKSHOP MANUAL:
C.92, CS.92, CB.92, C.95 & CA.95

HONDA 50cc FACTORY WORKSHOP MANUAL: C.100

HONDA 50cc FACTORY WORKSHOP MANUAL: C.110

HONDA (BOOK OF) MAINTENANCE & REPAIR 1960-1966:
50cc C.100, C.102, C.110 & C.114 ~ 125cc C.92 & CB.92
250cc C.72 & CB.72 ~ 305cc CB.77

LAMBRETTA (BOOK OF) MAINTENANCE & REPAIR:
125 & 150cc, all models up to 1958, except model "48".

NORTON FACTORY TWIN CYLINDER WORKSHOP MANUAL
1957-1970: *Lightweight Twins:* 250cc Jubilee, 350cc Navigator and 400cc Electra and the *Heavyweight Twins:* Model 77, 88, 88SS, 99, 99SS, Sports Special, Manxman, Mercury, Atlas, G15, P11, N15, Ranger (P11A).

NORTON (BOOK OF) MAINTENANCE & REPAIR 1932-1939:
All Pre-War SV, OHV and OHC models: 16H, 16I, 18, 19, 20, 50, 55, ES2, CJ, CSI, International 30 & 40

SUZUKI 200 & 250cc FACTORY WORKSHOP MANUAL:
250cc T20 [X-6 Hustler] ~ 200cc T200 [X-5 Invader & Sting Ray Scrambler]

SUZUKI 250cc FACTORY WORKSHOP MANUAL: 250cc ~ T10

TRIUMPH (BOOK OF) MAINTENANCE & REPAIR 1935-1939:
All Pre-War single & twin cylinder models: L2/1, 2/1, 2/5, 3/1, 3/2, 3/5, 5/1, 5/2, 5/3, 5/4, 5/5, 5/10, 6/1, Tiger 70, 80, 90 & 2H. Tiger 70C, 3S & 3H, Tiger 80C & 5H, Tiger 90C, 6S, 2HC & 3SC, 5T & 5S and T100

TRIUMPH 1937-1951 WORKSHOP MANUAL (A. St. J. Masters):
Covers rigid frame and sprung hub single cylinder SV & OHV and twin cylinder OHV pre-war, military, and post-war models

TRIUMPH 1945-1955 FACTORY WORKSHOP MANUAL NO.11:
Covers pre-unit, twin-cylinder rigid frame, sprung hub, swing-arm and 350cc, 500cc & 650cc.

VESPA (BOOK OF) MAINTENANCE & REPAIR 1946-1959:
All 125cc & 150cc models including 42/L2 & Gran Sport

VINCENT WORKSHOP MANUAL 1935-1955:
All Series A, B & C Models

COMING SOON IN THIS SAME SERIES:

BRIDGESTONE FACTORY WORKSHOP MANUAL: 50 Sport, 60 Sport, 90 De Luxe, 90 Trail, 90 Mountain, 90 Sport, 175 Dual Twin & Hurricane

BRITISH MILITARY MAINTENANCE & REPAIR MANUAL:
Service & Repair data for all British WD motorcycles

BRITISH MOTORCYCLE ENGINES: By the staff of "The Motor Cycle"

CEZETTA 175cc MODEL 501 SCOOTER MANUAL & PARTS BOOK

VILLIERS ENGINE WORKSHOP MANUAL: All Villiers engines through 1947

Please check our
website:

www.VelocePress.com

for a complete
up-to-date list of
available titles

Lightning Source UK Ltd.
Milton Keynes UK
UKOW05f2116010615

252720UK00001B/8/P